SONG TITLE SERIES

THE

BEACH BOYS

JOAN MAGUIRE

Copyright Page

New Beach Boys

Author: Joan Maguire

National Library of Australia Cataloguing-in-Publication – Publication entry

Author:	Maguire, Joan
Title:	Beach Boys / Joan Maguire.
ISBN:	978-0-9808551-4-2
Series:	Song title series
Subjects:	Beach Boys
	Beach Boys (Musical group)
	Rock musicians--United States--Biography
	Rock groups--United States--Biography

Dewey Number: 782.42166

Published with the assistance of: Love of Books and is available through the Print on Demand network and www.songtitleseries.com

This book is also available in a large print format and an E-book.

This soft cover short story book was created and written
By Joan Maguire on 14th September 2010 ©
ISBN: 978-0-9808551-4-2

E-book re-written April 2014© and is available through
the providers listed on www.songtitleseries.com
EISBN: 978-0-9925964-0-8

The large print book was created in March 2015 © and is available
through the same distributors as the normal book and
www.ssongtitleseries.com
ISBN: 978-0-9941998-9-8

DEDICATION

I would like to dedicate this book and say to thank you to my Earth Angel David and his friends, who inspire and motivate me to achieve things that I never dreamt, were possible.

INTRODUCTION

This book is another of the Song Title Series books. As I have enjoyed the challenge of writing these books, I hope that you will enjoy reading them.

The Beach Boys were a big part of my youth so I have used a total of 860 song titles (Italicized) to make this story possible. Legally I can not use Lyrics or Music because of Copyright but I can use song titles. Also due to the nature of my books; legally I must place a Reference (exactly as it is down loaded) and Bibliography in the back of the book.

Follow part of Marcella's life as she leaves school and starts her work experience program that takes her away from home to a different life and new lifelong friends like *Wendy* and *Barbara-Ann*. She is supported along the way by her father, a male friend and a mysterious *old master painter*, who turns out to be more than that.

When reading this "Song Title Series" book, I hope that no disservice has been done to the band as well as their adoring fans who read it, for that was not my intention. As I may have missed a song, an album or a concert within this book I do apologize sincerely. I have created and written this story without the sanctity of the band and I hope that if they read this they will enjoy it as well.

Well sit back and enjoy it and don't forget that because of using the original song titles in whole, there are places in the book that could be changed to make it more comprehensible for you the reader.

ACKNOWLEDGEMENTS

I would like to thank my daughters, Jenny and Kylie for their positive but critical input in the first draft of this book and all the help and support that they have given me throughout the Song Title Series books. With taking their input to mind, I have improved the book.

I would also like to thank my son Peter and his family for their support and help in keeping me grounded.

I would like to thank Kay and Julie for their patience and understanding whilst teaching me and giving me the skills to present my unique books in the best way possible.

I would also like to thank everyone else who has helped me bring this book to life and to you for purchasing it.

OTHER BOOKS IN THE SONG TITLE SERIES

Bon Jovi – Wanted Dead Or Alive
Green Day
Beach Boys
Slim Dusty
Country Women
Five Country Men
Six Crooners
Three Crooners
ABBA
The Rat Pack
Elton John
Classic 50s & 60s Rock 'N' Roll

CONTENTS

AT HOME

Once there was a *Tallahassee lassie* named *Marcella*, a farmer's daughter, who grew up living on a farm near the *Mount Vernon and Fairway* mountain range that ran along the *cotton fields* territory.

All summer long she would help in the *cotton fields*, milk *Mrs. O'Leary's cow* and go to school on *school days*. Some weekends, she would walk down to the *Ol' Man River* and just *be still* while listening to the *Okie from Muskogee*, who was an *old master painter*, recite the *Ballad of ol' Betsy* or the poem of *A Day in the Life of a Tree* that she almost knew off by heart. Sometimes they would just sit and talk about the olden day *heroes and villains* or play the game of *Roll Plymouth Rock* that he had made up for her when she was just a child.

One day, he told her "I was in a *bull session with big daddy* when we heard the news of a very bad accident on *Desert Drive*. My brother, Mickey, was *in my car*, a *little Honda* that he had borrowed, so he and his *friends* could go to the *county fair* that was just a bit to far to walk to. That *Friday night* whilst driving home, the *bright lights* of an oncoming truck blinded him and he had the accident.

Anna Lee, the healer was first on the scene and told him that *H.E.L.P. is on the way*, as he was trapped in the car. As was the case in any emergency, the townsfolk rallied around to give assistance to the emergency personnel who attended. Dad and I got there before the help arrived and were horrified to see that it was Mickey who was injured.

Naturally we ran to the car and asked him what happened but he couldn't remember anything except the bright lights. I knew that he was trapped and badly injured so I said to him *"Hold on dear brother and don't talk."* but he started to *cry* because *he couldn't get his poor body to move.*

Like a brother should, I tried to comfort and reassure him that *it's ok;* he was going to be alright. I even tried to make him laugh by saying *"Hang onto your ego* and if we have to, *we'll run away* together." or I'd say *"Let's go trippin', let's go away for awhile.* I know let's *go to heaven in my car."*

He spent the next three months in hospital and one day not long after he was released from hospital and *back home* and *all dressed up for school;* he told me that he felt dizzy. I said that he had *better get back into bed* but he collapsed and was taken back to the hospital.

He died from the lack of *oxygen to the brain* and he was buried in *Hully Gully*, as it was his favorite place to watch the masses of flying *bluebirds over the mountain* and where he would *let the wind blow* through his hair.

I'm bugged at my ol' man 'cos *love and mercy* were not in him and he carried on with his life just as if nothing had happened. Now *my hobo heart* is like *Frosty the Snowman*, a *child of winter* because *I just wasn't made for these times* of continually *livin' with a heartache* caused by the loss of my brother and my *looking back with love* for him. That was the *matchpoint of our love* and *still I dream of it* happening all over again."

Later that afternoon and back in the *barnyard, Marcella* finished her chores and went in for supper which was finished off with her favorite Cherry and Chocolate Pie with freshly whipped cream.

During the evening and whilst completing her studies, she listened to the *radio station jingles* and laughed when the announcer asked "*Do you like worms*? Well, *do you like worms*? Well, if you do, then *TM Song* has a new range of *Wild Honey* candy. *Wild Honey* is collected in the valley below the *Mount Vernon and Fairway* mountain range. *Too much sugar* can be bad for you, so try eating honey based products instead. Look out for them in the store nearest to you."

The *cuckoo clock* woke her the following morning and as she got ready for school, she could hear the *pet sounds* coming from the *barnyard*; like *Mrs. O'Leary's cow*, the cute little piglets and a *little bird* whistling a tune outside her window.

"Now." she said to herself "Do I have *everything I need* for school?"

At the bus stop, the *little children* were usually accompanied by an older sibling or a parent or guardian. She had to smile to herself as one *mama says* to her elder son "Now, I have to go or I'll be late for work and don't you let *him run wild* or run on the road." before they boarded the bus that would *chug-a-lug* down the road towards more children and the school.

On the bus, she reread the *narrative: Cinco De Mayo* and the *narrative: Venice Beach*, that she would need to know for her lessons this week but next week she needed to know the *narrative: Between Picture* for Tuesday and the *narrative: Room with a view* for next Thursday.

She knew that her *graduation day*, at the end of the semester, wouldn't take very long to come around so she really needed to brush up on school work for the exams.

Her concentration was broken by "*Caroline, no. Orange Crate art* is not anything special. The picture of the *Palm Tree and Moon* is a classic *of the times* it was painted in." she heard *Marilyn Rovell* say.

"Has anyone here read the novels by D.B.*Medley*: *Talk To Me, Baby Blue* or *Please Let Me Wonder* lately?" asked Karen.

She noticed a new house being erected and a couple of new signs for a new housing estate. "*This town goes down at sunset,* so not much happens here at night so why would people want to move out here. It's a good thing that *Whistle In* City is only ten miles east of the cotton fields." she thought as she looked out the bus window towards the mountains that loomed over the cotton fields.

The bus jerked to a stop at the school gate at *409 Auld Lang Syne Road Skatetown U.S.A.* which was four miles from where she lived.

"*Help me, Rhonda.*" asked the bus driver as a child was struggling to get off the bus. "If he tries to get off on his own, we will be here *all summer long* or maybe *'til I die.*"

The school bell rang and the children shouted to each other, "*Run don't walk* to class or you'll be late."

As the young children started to run to class, *Marcella* thought "*Their hearts were full of spring* but would they still be that way when they get to the higher classes in years to come."

4

STUDENT PLANS

The exams had finished and it was two weeks before *graduation day*, when *Susie Cincinnati*, senior Fundraising Chair person decided that it was a good time for the graduating students to put on a final *student demonstration time* and arranged for a *toy drive public service announcement* to be done.

Susie said that you have to *be true to your school* motto and help those in need, and as *Christmas time is here again* in a couple of months, we should do something for the community, like putting on the play *O Holy Night* or hold a concert.

The other students said "The play, let's not *do it again* this year. Let's do the concert."

Susie arranged with the local radio station for a fellow student to go and give his speech; his *Denis Wilson Christmas message* to all the local and surrounding citizens about their toy drive and concert.

The students arranged to put on a concert at *Palisade Park* for the younger children and their families and to give a Christmas toy gift to all the children under the age of twelve years of age. Teenagers should understand why they were not eligible to receive a toy. The *concert promo* was advertised in a way to make everyone feel *Christmasey*.

It was during a *Brian Wilson interview*, that a *little girl intro* was made and she was asked what she wanted for Christmas. She sadly replied "*What I really want for Christmas* is for my *papa-oom-mow-mow* to come home so he can hear the *bells of Christmas* on *Christmas day*. Every year *papa-oom-mow-mow* says "*I'll be home for Christmas*." but he never gets here. I guess that we will have another *blue Christmas* without him."

A young boy was asked what he wanted and he replied "*Santa Clause is coming to town* soon. I hope *Santa's got an airplane* in his big sack for me, 'cos *when I grow up to be a man*, I want to be a pilot or maybe he will have some *games two can play* with outside.

Mom says that it's good when my brother and I play outside but he can't play some of the games I like to play because he's too little. I will leave some cookies and milk *in my room* for Santa and I hope that too many crumbs don't get caught in *Santa's beard*."

Susie Cincinnati and a few other students arranged to *add some music* to the day so they contacted a few agents asking for their help to get a big named band to play at their concert; arranged for the church choir to sing *God Rest You Merry Gentlemen, Hark The Herald Angels Sing* and *It Came Upon A Midnight Clear* and the school orchestra to play *The Waltz, The First Noel* and *The Lord's Prayer*.

They asked *Big Sur* if he would play Santa for the day.

Meanwhile, *Brian Wilson* had an idea and said "Please will you *help me, Rhonda*. I spoke to the little girl's mother about papa-oom-mow-mow and her daughter's wish and she gave me some information to his whereabouts and contact details. If *I get around* to our car club headquarters and contact the guys and girls, then maybe I'll be able to get our team working to find him and see if he would like to see his family this Christmas. I will need your help once we contact him."

They never had much trouble finding papa, whose real name was *Johnny Carson*, but he was not sure if he could make it back home. His ship, *The Sloop John B.* was getting ready to sail away from *San Francisco* to the *South American* city of *San Miguel* and then from *San Miguel* to *Sumahama* which is somewhere near Japan I think. Johnny said that it was a four month trip but after Rhonda had spoken to him, he changed his mind and was coming home. *God only knows how she boogalooed it*, but she did.

"If you could *be here in the morning*, of the concert, that would be great. It would be easier for us to arrange for *Brian* to meet you on the *Saturday morning in the city* bus station car park." said Rhonda.

He said "*I just got my pay* so I could travel there from *Salt Lake City*. The *country air* might give me the *country feelin'* back again. *Being with the one you love*, especially at Christmas is important to a child.

I always said that *when I grow up to be a man*, I will always spend Christmas with my family but in the last few years, unfortunately I have been somewhere else in the world and couldn't make it back in time. Really this is *where I belong* at Christmas, with my family."

Early, on the Saturday morning of the concert, everyone knew that they didn't have that much *time* to get everything ready because of the *concert tonight*, which really started late in the afternoon, would soon be upon them.

6

"*Caroline, No*. You can't play *trombone Dixie* tonight, it's not a Christmas type tune." said Susie.

Then she turned to *Big Sur* and said "*Are you ready* for today because the children will have to believe that you really are *the man with all the toys.*"

At one stage Susie said "*I just wasn't made for these times*, I feel as if I'm *getting in over my head* with all the organizing and *there's so many things* that still have to be done. Will you *help me, Rhonda* please", and handed her a list with some of the running around that needs to be done on it?"

Now as planned before hand, Susie reminded everyone of their duties for the day. "*Johnny B. Goode*, you are the M.C. for the afternoon and evening and besides announcing the entertainment we have organized, I have just had confirmation that the band, *The Beaks Of Eagles*, the *Grammy winners*, will be here around six o'clock and will play their latest hit *Winter Symphony* and the *Monster Mash*, a *song for children.*

Terry, you are the *little Saint Nick* at the South stand, making sure that there is *cool, cool water* for everyone to drink and Roy, you are the *little Saint Nick* handing out the *shortenin' bread* over there. Frank, you are the *little Saint Nick* at the North stand, making sure that there is *cool, cool water* for everyone to drink and Tommy, you are the *little Saint Nick* handing out the *shortenin' bread* over there. Billy, you are the *little Saint Nick* that's helping Santa with his sacks. Thank you, guys.

Faye and Karen, you are the *Disney girls* ushering the people to their seats from the Southern entrance and Diane and Louise you are the *Disney girls* doing the same on the Northern entrance. Thank you, girls."

The crowds started gathering around the stands to get their drinks and shortenin' bread and the entrances, with some people already seated inside. Outside the north entrance some young children ran to their parents saying excitedly, "*The man with the toys* is here. *I saw Santa rockin' around the Christmas tree* singing *We Three Kings Of Orient Are* in a funny voice. Will he do it again at our place at Christmas time?"

It was about five o'clock when the *concert intro* was made, followed by the *band intro*.

As they started playing *Rockin' All Over The World*, someone called out to Susie and Rhonda *"Brian's Back."*

Susie hurried over to Brian and said *"It's about time* you got here. Where have you been and where's Johnny?"

Brian replied "I had to park my *little deuce coupe* way back *in the parkin' lot* because someone parked their *little Honda* over the *lines* and took up two car parks, Johnny's changing in the club's *workshop* and is right behind me."

The afternoon and evening ran smoothly and all the children received a toy and the last gift given was to the little girl who with her family also received an extra special gift, her papa-oom-mow-mow.

The little girl said "Mommy said that God will answer *our prayer* if we believe in him."

Johnny had asked to keep his arrival a secret from the family so it would be a Christmas surprise for all of them.

At the *end of the show*, Susie thanked her fellow students for all their hard work and the help given by the other people involved, she thanked the people for their support and for turning up and then she said that on behalf of the school, we hope that you all have had a *good time* and *we wish you a Merry Christmas.*

THE LETTER

On *Christmas Day, Marcella* said "*Morning Christmas.*" got dressed and then went down stairs where her father greeted her with "*Merry Christmas baby.*"

He had spent yesterday trying to *deck the halls* with colorful decorations as well as putting up the Christmas tree. He also slipped a special present under the tree for Mrs. O'Leary with a note saying "Thank you for being *good to my baby* while she was growing up."

Over breakfast, her father said "*Let's go away for a while, on a holiday*. We could go down and have *summer in Monterey* instead of a *white Christmas here.*

Now that you've had your *graduation day*, you'll be *leaving this town* soon to go on your work exchange program, I'll have to stop thinking of you as *the little girl I once knew. Walking down the path of life* means that sometimes *you need a mess of help to stand alone*, so remember that I'm here and so is Mrs. O'Leary if you ever need someone or something. Now let's talk about our holiday."

Marcella's father said that they could book into a place called *Kokomo* where they could be *busy doin' nothing* and have some *hot fun in the summertime* and they could go to the *Cabinessence* café for a *Funky Pretty Ding Dang*; an ice-cream soda made with different kinds of fruits, ice-creams, toppings and different kinds of nuts.

Marcy said "*Wouldn't it be nice* if Mrs. O'Leary could come with us. She doesn't have any family to be with except us."

Her father replied "Not this *time*, I want this holiday *only with you* and I have made arrangements for a different holiday for Mrs. O'Leary."

They spent the rest of the morning making their travel plans and that afternoon, when, *after the game* on the television that they both had watched was finished, Marcella's father watched the *"Cassius" Love vs 'Sonny' Wilson* fight on the telly, so Marcella took her *magic transistor radio* and went down to the *Ol' Man River* to visit the old master painter who was cooking some meat in the coals and some *vegatables* on his campfire outside his cabin.

She enjoyed going to the cabin because on one side of the walls under a wide tin roof, carefully hung several of his paintings that he called his *"Unreleased Backgrounds."* of his old world and some *wind chimes* that sent out *good vibrations* when they rang from the blowing wind.

By the front door, also under a wide tin roof, was a roughly made table and around that were large logs made into chairs. A narrower tin roof was covering the other two walls and near the back door was a veggie patch where several seasonal veggies grew and a chicken coop with two chickens that laid eggs for the painter everyday. Another shed nearby that looked like an unusual barn housed a cow that supplied his daily quota of milk.

A dog started barking and when he saw her coming, the old painter said *"Lay down Burden*, it's only Marcella.

Hey little tomboy, take a load off your feet, let *the warmth of the sun* shine down on us awhile and *let the wind blow* a soft breeze while we spend some time together.

You know, I remember when *you love to say Da Da* all the time and when you loved to hear a *fairy tale* and listen to *fairy tale music* and *dance, dance, dance.*

Now look at you, you've turned into a beautiful young *lady."*

"Yes." said Marcella "It *seems so long ago* now, and *I love to say Da Da* still, but just as a tease. Now dad just laughs and says *kiss me baby* and *how's about a little bit of your sweet lovin'."*

Marcella wished him a merry Christmas and gave him the small gift that she had especially made for him.

During the afternoon, she spoke about *goin' south* for the holiday with her father and then the forth coming work exchange program where she would spend three months in *Hawaii* and three months in *California.*

"All I want to do is get a decent job that will allow me to help dad because he won't be able to run the farm on his own in a few years time and Mrs. O'Leary will be retiring soon." said Marcella.

The afternoon slipped by so quickly and when she left, the old painter said *"Farewell my friend.* Enjoy your *summer in paradise* and have nothing but *fun, fun, fun* on your holiday and as far as the work exchange program, always *believe in yourself* that you will succeed because you are one of the *smart girls* in this town who will *make it big*.

Remember, that God in *heaven* hears *our prayer* every time we pray and he will answer you, but maybe not in the way you expect.

He says that if *you still believe in me*, especially when things go wrong, I will either show you the way to get back on the right track or I will send someone to help you find your way."

The following morning, *Brian* had agreed to drive Marcella and her father to Whistle In City in his *little deuce coupe* so that they could catch the *409 airplane* to Monterey that afternoon to start their holiday together.

At the airport, just before he left to drive back home, Brian handed Marcella a letter to read on the plane.

In the letter Brian wrote "*A friend like you* will be missed. *Just once in my life* I wish that I hadn't kept *a thing or two* to myself. You are now on that *airplane* heading for a new life after your holiday. *In my room* and *in the still of the night I'll remember* the *roller skating child* that you once were, the times we shared ice-cream sodas at *The Monkey's Uncle* Diner and the *things we did last summer*.

I have kept these things and more to myself because *when girls get together*, gossip spreads and they would have laughed and made fun of me.

I used to tell myself "*You've got to hide your love away*." even though *that's not me* and because *I'm so young*, I didn't know how to tell you about *what you do to me*. I was also worried about *what you gonna do about me* if I told you.

My sister, *Peggy Sue* knows that I like you a lot but I know that she never said anything to you, not even as a *passing friend* because she knows too that *when girls get together* and start talking, they can be so cruel with their gossip.

Maybe I don't know if I was *meant for you* but I wish you could *be my baby* and give me some of your *good vibrations*. *God only knows* when I will see you again but *that lucky old sun* will always shine down on you.

11

Don't back down on your aspirations, hopes and dreams.

If I could talk to love then *I wish for you* all the happiness that *this whole world* could give you and *I wanna pick you up* whenever you get down, so I will be here when you need a friend. *Love ya*, Brian."

DAD'S SECRET

They arrived in Monterey and were soon booked into the *Kokomo* Hotel that had a casual look and feel about it. There were several themed suites that guests could stay in; like the Valentino suite, which was decorated in a very conservative, old fashioned way, or the Western suite that had a picture of *ten little Indians* hanging on the wall opposite the entrance door or the *Seasons In The Sun* suite that they were going to be staying in.

That afternoon they spent exploring the town in *the warmth of the sun* and when evening came, her father took her to the *Cabinessence* café where he bought her a *Funky Pretty Ding Dang*; an ice-cream soda that was made from bananas, passionfruit and pineapple and was delicious.

They sat in silence for awhile, and then her father said "*Darlin'*, I know that we don't speak about your mother very often; however, now that you've grown up, I am going to tell you about your mother; the whole story.

Your mother was a *Mexican girl* and we met right here at the *Cabinessence* café. She wanted to *breakaway* from her life of just work, work, work and become one of the *California girls*.

One night I rented a *little Honda* and I picked her up from her second job and we went *honkin' down the highway* to *Blueberry Hill*, the *mountain of love* and something *wonderful* happened there that night.

The following week when she had her day off we went by train to *Diamond Head*, and I *remember walking in the sand* before we sat *under the boardwalk* where I looked into her *rainbow eyes* and said "*I do love you.*" and I proposed to her, *then I kissed her.*

I should have known better at the time than to get married so quickly, but we did get married in the *Chapel of Love* and a year later you were born.

We moved back to the farm to live with my parents but your mother was still *California dreaming*, however, she fell pregnant again and had a baby boy, Denny.

My parents as you know passed on just after we arrived back at the farm so I think that being in a strange place, having two babies to care for and the farm were too much for her and one night in my room (*ganz allein*) as she would say, she told me "I wasn't *meant for you*." and that she was leaving but only taking our son with her and leaving you here with me.

Our sweet love was over but I think now that *givin' you up* was the best thing she did, because as Denny grew, she *let him run wild*.

Then she met a *long tall Texan* and went to live on his ranch. Denny was always told "*don't go near the water*." but one day he went missing and after a long search they found *Denny's drums* on the edge of the river and his body further down, snagged on a log.

He was three years old when he drowned, on the *4th of July*. Your mother told me he used to pretend to play the *river song, Sail on Sailor* on the drums that I had sent him for Christmas.

Not long after the death of our son she got the *California calling* again and left the Texan, the ranch and Texas behind and moved to where she had always wanted to be but a *California saga* started between us.

I *got to know the woman* better and realized what life would have be like if I tried to *hold on* to her, so in the end I said to her "*Heads you win, tails I lose*" and I gave up trying to *hold back time. Everybody wants to live* and have *fun, fun, fun* but she didn't want to be with us anymore.

Do you remember when you were ten and I went away for a week? well, your mother had become very ill and during the week I was away, she died.

Just before she died she said to me "Marcella, *don't let her know she's an angel I'm begging you please*, don't ever tell her that I said that to you."

I told her that after you graduate, I would bring you here and tell you the truth about your mother and your deceased brother because you have a right to know and you would be old enough to understand.

All the *amusement parks USA* that you could bring to the town couldn't make me feel any better in my heart because *I was made to love her*, I think I will love her *'til I die*.

I went to sleep that night *thinkin' 'bout you baby*."

As she took her father's hand, Marcella said softly "It must have been hard for you to keep this secret from me for all these years. *Do you have any regrets?*"

Her father replied "Sometimes, because *a young man is gone* but *don't you worry baby* because my love and my life have been *devoted to you* making sure that you have everything you need and it always will be *'til I die*. Remember *darlin', never learn not to love* and don't become a *dreamer*.

You can never answer the question *why do fools fall in love* or know *what love can do* to you or the other person. If love is going to happen it will and you can't do anything about it but take it slowly until you are really sure that it is right for you and the other person.

Come go with me, back to the hotel, *it's getting late* so let's go and get some sleep because tomorrow we're going to have nothing but *fun, fun, fun*."

Back at the hotel Marcella sat in her room trying to understand everything her father had told her. She had a little brother who was now buried in Texas somewhere. Her mother had abandoned her, leaving her with her father, but why? But most importantly how was her father feeling now, upset, relieved, depressed? He had not answered the question when she had asked.

Now, with her work exchange program which meant that she would have to leave home, would her father be able to cope or would he just give up?

She would talk to her father about it in a few days time because he needed to have his time with her and all the fun and laughter that they could have together.

Just before she drifted off to sleep, she thought that someone said to her "Both you and your father will be alright. It takes time to heal but you both have a new life waiting for you and old friends to catch up with who will help you."

NEW FRIENDS

The holiday came to an end and Marcella and her father drove to the airport where he would fly back to Whistle In City, where Brian would pick him up and take him home, and she would fly to *Hawaii*, for the first three months of the work exchange program.

On the plane, Marcella thought back to the conversation with her father that she had had in the *Cabinessence* café about her mother and her little brother and the way her father had spoken about her mother. I think dad will love mom in his own way *forever* and I think he may have said to her many times, "*You don't have to hang on to your ego, Angel come home, I do* love you, please, don't *let us go on this way*, we can work things out. Maybe we can get someone in to help you while you settle in."

If there were any *heroes and villains* in his *California saga* with mom, then I think that dad would be the hero. In many ways I can see now why he kept it a secret until now; however, I know now that mom can never *tell me why* she left but I wish that I could have grown up with my little brother, Denny.

One day I will have to go to Texas and visit his grave. I wonder if that picture of the little boy that dad has is Denny?"

The plane touched down in Hawaii and a woman named *Misirlou*, or Lou as she was known by, was waiting for her and some other girls who arrived shortly after she had.

In the group, there were some *belles of Paris*, a couple of *California girls* and *the girl from New York City*, named Lizzy. Lou welcomed them all, and then they boarded a small bus that took them to the apartments where they would spend the next three months.

As they arrived at the *Melekalikmaka* Apartments, she noticed the address, *409 Auld Lang Syne* Avenue and she immediately thought about her old high school, that had the same address and remembered the school motto; always *be true to your school* motto and help people in need.

After settling into their own little rooms, that had a single bed, a built-in closet and a small desk/ table and a chair with a coral looking reading lamp on it and an arm chair to just sit and relax in, the girls spent the rest of the day exploring the city.

Marcella and the two *California girls*, *Barbara-Ann* and *Wendy* were in town together when they heard someone shout "*Surf's up.*"

Both of the other girls looked at each other and said "*Let's go.*"

Wendy turned to Marcella and said "I'm a *surfer girl* and *surfin' USA* is a dream of mine. I would love to have the money to go on a *surfin' safari*, so if I work hard and save, then my dreams may come true."

The girls raced back to the hotel to change and then quickly headed for the beach.

That lucky old sun grew even *hotter* as they day progressed but the girls still had a great time down at the beach. Wendy borrowed a board and paddled out to *catch a wave* where she did a couple of manoeuvres called *loop de loop* and *Alley Oop* and because she was a goofy foot surfer, left foot in front, she was able to do the moves easily.

The waves just kept coming *on and on and on* and Wendy, would *do it again* and again, paddle out then ride the waves back in.

On the horizon, Marcy could just make out the silhouette shape of the *Sloop John B* heading for port.

Marcella thought "*Wouldn't it be nice* to have grown up near the ocean. *That lucky old sun* just drifts in the sky all day long passing over *this whole world* on its never-ending journey. *The warmth of the sun* makes me think that *today* is not the *time to get alone* in a small stuffy apartment room."

"*Help me, Rhonda* to put some sunscreen on my back and *girl don't tell me* I don't need it?" Marcella heard a young man say.

The surfer moon started creeping up on the horizon and someone down the beach shouted "*Here comes the night. Do you wanna dance*? The local band *Love and Mercy* will be playing up at the point in an hour. *I can hear music* coming from there even now."

Even though the girls were tired from their travels, they decided that as *the night was so young*, they would go and see one of the shows that were playing in town. *Please Let Me Wonder* sounded boring so they chose to go to see *Shut Down* and during the *show intro*, they realized that they were getting hungry.

17

Because of all the excitement of the day, none of the girls had eaten, so after the show they went to a diner that was situated half way between theatre and their apartment, for a burger.

They all agreed that *Shut Down* was such a good show that they would have to go and see *Shut Down Part II* when it comes out.

Back in her room, Marcy, as the girls called her, took out her journal and started writing. She had so much to write about and in her description of the girls she had spent the day with, she wrote *"Their hearts were full of spring* and *life is for the living* while you're still young. These two *California girls* send out *good vibrations* to everyone they meet and even though it may be *too early to tell,* I hope that we remain close friends while I'm here and when I have to spend the time in California."

As *the night was so young* still and Marcy was feeling a bit tired, she laid on her bed listening to the local radio station and thought *"Gee,* I hope dad is going to be alright. I hate being away from him now that he needs somebody to fill his *silent night.* Tomorrow Mrs. O'Leary will be there for him if he needs her. I wonder if she knew about mom and dad."

She had a giggle to herself when she heard the announcer say *"This song wants to sleep with you tonight."* and played the *Love and Mercy* song *This Isn't Love.*

WORK AND PLAY

The following morning, all the girls on the work exchange program met in the organization's office that was situated just four blocks uptown from where they were staying, where they were informed of their work locations.

In the large brightly light office were ten desks and chairs, one each for the work exchange participants, a large white board and a very long table that had books, name tags and pens and small note books on it. On the walls behind the desks were hanging some beautiful prints of the Hawaiian Islands and some interesting saying and mottos.

Lou told the girls that their work experience placements would be according to their first application work selections so Lizzy, the girl from New York was employed with *Lady Lynda* in her *Lahaina Aloha* Fashion Boutique a few streets away.

Barbara-Ann was given employment at the *Pet Sounds* Recording Studio and shop. Wendy was placed at the *Noble Surfer* and Marcy was placed as a receptionist at *Radio King Dom*.

They each went with an escort on their separate ways for the day but when they got together in the evening, they all talked about their respective work and what it entailed. Lizzy just grumbled something and stormed out the room stating that she was tired and was going to bed.

Barbara-Anne said "I like this job. *I get around* to all the studios and I get to meet bands like *Melt Away, Love and Mercy* and *Moon Dawg*; they all play *rock and roll music. Melt Away* was in today and they told me that *"our favorite recording sessions* are done here because of the relaxed atmosphere and the professional people who work here."

My job entails doing *all this is that*. You know what I mean, like showing the clients to the recording studios, making sure that they have everything they need, answering phones and recording the written procedures of the recording sessions given to me by the session manager on the computer *in my room*. That's right I have my own little office which they call rooms.

Coming here on this program was *good timin'* for me because the girl who was doing this job went on an overseas holiday for three months and

19

if I do well here, the boss will recommend me for a job in their studios back in California.

The best thing though is *I can hear music* all day long especially Moon Dawg's new single, *Island girl*. The melody is so catchy."

Wendy said "My boss is known as *Trader* and he's a *South Bay surfer*. He told me that he was a *problem child* when he was younger and had run away to sea. He got a job as a deck hand on the *Sloop John B*. and had sailed with the *Santa Ana winds* to *San Miguel* but the worst part was sailing *full sail* home again against the *Santa Ana winds* which was pretty scary, but the pay was good. He only did five trips and had saved enough money to buy his surfboard shop.

He said he also tried being *the baker man* on a *steamboat*, but he wasn't good at that job, so he tried to be the D.J. He tried *rocking the man in the boat* but that ended up as a *no-go showboat* because the captain only wanted to hear the *river song, Sail On Sailor*.

In the end he decided to take a chance and open up his own surf business by making, selling or hiring out boards to the public. His business has taken off and in the near future he intends to expand it so he is looking at other places.

Trader is teaching me all about boards, how to make them, look after them and which ones to use in different types of surf. Naturally we have to try the boards out and he was extremely pleased with the way I can surf.

Tomorrow we are *looking down the coast* and if the *water builds up* in the right direction, then he is going to strap a few boards to his *cherry cherry coupe* and we are going *surfin'*. He calls me his *little surfer girl*.

I think that I could really get to love this job. You know I think I could keep surfing *'til I die.*"

Marcy said "*I'll bet he's nice* and will be a good person to work for, but I don't have such an exciting job as you two; however, I do get to speak to some interesting people there.

The lifestyle here is so different to the cotton fields where I grew up and *still I dream of it* and all the farm animals as well.

20

Everything and everyone is in a hurry here and I have never heard of some of these bands that are due to come in this week for radio interviews.

Hushabye is coming Wednesday for the *Morning Beat* show, *Melt Away* on Thursday to talk about their new album and *Heroes and Villains* are coming in on Friday.

The music played on our radio station back home sounds like a *lullaby* to what you listen to here in the big cities. I feel so out of place that I want to run to *the nearest faraway place* that I can find and just hide there."

They were interrupted when someone asked "Have you seen *lazy Lizzy*, the one who thinks she's a *calendar girl* and who wants everyone to wait on her?"

They all shook their heads to say no.

Barbara-Ann said "*Don't worry baby*, Wendy and I will help you. I think that if we go and spend some time in your town, we would feel out of place there ourselves. What we need to do, is go out every night for awhile and have some *fun, fun, fun* and *dance, dance, dance* so you get used to our music and way of life and we can teach you about the bands.

Don't forget that *midnight's another day* so *looking at tomorrow* now is just a waste of time because tomorrow never comes. Just *live let live, here today.*"

Marcy said "Can you *teach me tonight* a little bit about Hushaby because they are coming in to the station first?"

DAD'S REPLY

Marcy, Barbara-Ann and Wendy became really good friends and the two girls taught Marcy all about music and the city way of life. Marcy wrote to her father often, telling him all about her work and the many other experiences that she had had since her last letter to him.

She wrote "Wendy has taught me to surf, *the first time* I tried to get on the board; I just rolled right over it, which must have been a funny sight. Then when I did start standing up, I used to *wipe out* (fall off) quite often but I soon learnt to stay on the board otherwise the waves will wash you in one direction and the board in another direction, which makes it hard to retrieve.

So now Wendy calls me a *surfer girl* and will only allow me to surf near her until I can gain more experience to be able to head off on my own and I don't think that will be happening anywhere in the near future.

Barbara-Ann, because she is in the same sort of employment as me, has taught me all about the music scene and many of the bands that are still around and some of the new bands that are starting to break through; however, I think that *Heroes and Villains* has become my favorite and *Hushaby,* a new band over here, has left to tour Canada for two months, maybe my next favourite.

Sometimes when I'm *in my room* at night, I get the *city blues* because I miss everyone back there and I miss going down to look at *Sweet Mountain* that the River *Feel flows* from. I may be over here in *blue Hawaii* but I *still dream of it* and sometimes I have a few *tears in the morning.*

I guess that I will always be a country girl inside and will be *'til I die.* I also miss visiting the old master painter. Do you see much of the old master painter and my other school friends?

I'm waiting for the day that I can come home and visit for awhile. Love you dad. Marcella."

A week later when she arrived home from work, she received the letter from her father. As she walked up stairs to her *little pad,* she passed Lizzy and Caroline arguing on one of the walkways that were between the stairs connecting the floors and also near the elevators.

"*Caroline, no* I am not wearing a wig, this is my own hair. I have just done something different with it." said Lizzy before storming off.

Caroline whispered to me "With all that stuff she uses, *she's goin' bald* and has to hide it under a wig or hair piece but she won't admit it."

Once in her room she grabbed a drink, sat down in the comfy armchair and opened the letter from her father and read "*Darlin'*, I was a little sad after reading your last letter but *don't worry baby* and *don't back down* from this new experience. Maybe the city life is not *meant for you* but give it awhile to get used to it, then make up your mind.

I hadn't seen the old master painter for awhile so I went down to see him but he had gone. I think that after all these years living here in this town; he has become *the wanderer* again. *I get around* a little bit more than I used to, so I do see your friends and they often ask after you.

Pamela Jean is getting married to a young man from Whistle In City and will be on her honeymoon in San Francisco before the *fall breaks and back to winter* and the cold weather. *Mona* has work in the *Honky Tonk* Bar and Grill just outside town. I have spoken to her and she is not happy working there but she told me that she has almost earned enough money to pay the fees for her Business Degree that she wants to get next year.

Carl joined a theatre company and *Carl's big chance* is in a play called *Child is Father of the Man* or *Child is the Father of the Man*, well, which ever one it is, it's going to open *on Broadway* around May.

Susie, Rhonda, Karl and Paddy all told me how much they miss having you around and they told me to tell you to keep at it and enjoy yourself while you can. When you have the opportunity to come back for a holiday or for good, then they will catch up with you.

Do you remember that *car crazy cutie*, the *pom pom play girl* who was hanging around Brian, well, *it's over now*. She is now dating Joseph Banks and is working part time at the school.

Since you've been gone, Brian comes out here in his *little deuce coupe* quite often and he'll take me out for a drive somewhere, take me to town shopping or he'll just sit and talk, mainly about you.

When he's not here, he's helping out down in his club but I suppose that he'll tell you all about it in his letter that he has asked me to pass on to you.

Keep your chin up and remember I love you *and your dreams come true* if you believe in them. Love, Dad."

Then she opened Brian's letter "Dear Marcella, I guess that you have read your father's letter and know most of the gossip of the town.

I visit your father often because I know that he misses you more than your friends do. I also know that he occasionally needs an extra pair of hands at the farm. *Everyone's in love with you* back here and we all hope you *make it good* in the work that you are doing because of the *good vibrations* that you give.

Our team in *our car club* are working on a black *little deuce coupe* to make it a *custom machine* for the car show that is coming to the *drive-in* at Whistle In City in a months time. I have a cousin in California who customs cars and I have helped him in the past so we are trying to make this little car get noticed in a big way.

Your dad asked me if I knew of the bands *Heroes and Villains* and *Hushaby* and I told him that *Heroes and Villains* were a good band although we don't hear much of them but I hadn't heard of the other one.

I suggested to your father "*Let's go away for awhile* to the *Rio Grande* or *let's go trippin'* down the *long Promised Road* to the *Lonely Sea* camp site and go fishing," but I think that we would both would have got the *Pacific Ocean blues* with you being so far away *over the waves.*

Maybe I'm chasing *rainbows* that you and I can share a *sweet Sunday kinda love one* day. I can't help *thinkin' 'bout you baby* and wish that you were *with me tonight* because I didn't realize how you meant to me until you went away and I had to spend the *Monday without you.*

You'll be back in California in six weeks time and maybe you could get a chance to come home for a few days. *I'd love just once to see you* again. All my love. Brian."

Marcella was so surprised with the last part of the contents of Brian's letter. He had said something in his last letter that she had read on the plane about the way he felt about her but she had thought that *they're only words* coming from him because he was going around with Lana.

He has broken up with Lana and now, he tells me how he feels about me. So what can I do about it?

24

How do I feel about Brian?

That question is going to take some time to answer.

Thinking about it she had come to realize that he had spent more time with her over the last few years, although he had not really been more than a close friend to her and he had never shown or said anything to make her think differently.

Yes, she did like him a lot, but could it now become more than just a friendship?

Only time would tell.

TIME FLIES

That evening Marcy met up with Barbara Anne and Wendy at the diner where they often went to eat. The food at the restaurant section of the apartment was often not very nice and it always seems to be crowded and noisy due to the arguments between Lizzy and some of the other girl.

When she sat down in the booth Wendy asked "*What's wrong.* Have you had some bad news about your father?"

"No." said Marcy "he's alright." and then told them about Brian and how in his two letters that he had broken up with his girlfriend and that his ex-girlfriend was now dating someone else and how he now felt about her.

How he had been helping around the farm and spending time with her father and taking him out so that he was never able to get lonely for too long and how he was helping his car club customize a car for a local car show.

Barbara-Ann said "*I'll bet he's nice* and I'm getting *good vibrations* from what you've said and the way you've spoken of him. How do you feel about him?"

Before she could answer, the girls heard behind them "*Caroline, no.* Don't *do it again.* You have to eat your *vegetables*, not throw them around."

"But I don't like these *vega – tables*, they're yucky." a young girl replied.

The girls had a giggle over the reply and Wendy said "I didn't like veggies when I was young either. Mom and I often fought over it."

Then a little boy was heard saying "*When I grow up to be a man*, I'm going to grow my own vegetables and make you eat them Caroline."

"*Don't talk* with your mouth full." said the mother.

The next five weeks just seemed to fly by and during the last week, all the girls from the program had to meet in the organization's office to get feedback on their work placements.

Lou said "It seems that you *California girls* have done very well here and going home will be easy for you to continue your program."

Pet Sounds were so impressed with Barbara-Ann, that they made arrangements for her to continue her work exchange program back in California with a view that after the three months were finished, she would get full time employment with them.

Wendy's report was the same; however, she would become a *surfin'* instructor as well.

Through the earlier help received from the other two girls, Marcy received a glowing report and also a continuation of work in the sister station "The *Solar System* Station" in California, with the opportunity of advancement to learn more of the business when the program had finished.

Lizzy's report was not very good and finding her another placement back home was nigh on impossible. "Please *be here in the morning* so we can discuss your future in the program." said Lou.

As all the girls were leaving the office, they were each given an envelope that contained a letter for the next work experience employer, a certificate that stated that they had finished that part of the program and a letter to tell them where and to whom they were to report to when they got home or to their destinations.

Everyone was given the next two days to organize themselves for their return to their respective homes.

Wendy said "Let's go out and *celebrate the news.*"

Then she asked "Where in California are your placements?"

After opening their envelopes, they were all surprised to see that they would all be in *Koma* on the *Kona Coast* of *Southern California*, a two hour drive south of Los Angeles, and Wendy's home town.

Wendy was so excited that she immediately phoned her parents and said "I *had to phone ya* with the news that my new placement is back there at home and my two fiends have also got their placement back there in my home town."

Arrangements were made with her parents that the three girls would all move into and live in their summer house near the beach.

27

When Wendy told the other girls of the news she said "I can't wait for that plane to *carry me home*. Dad said that it's a *miracle* that the summer house just happens to be vacant now because the people who were renting it had a sudden change of plans and left yesterday."

Marcy rang her father and said "I *had to phone ya* with the news about my new placement and where I'd be living. *Wouldn't it be nice* if we could spend some time together more often when I get back? Could you please pass the news on to Brian for me as I think he would like to know? See you soon dad."

Barbara Anne also contacted her parents with the news of her next placement and agreed to catch up with her parents as soon as she could.

For their last night in Hawaii, the girls went to a club just down the street from the diner to listen and *dance, dance, dance* to the band *Heroes and Villains* and they made sure that the evening was one that they would never forget.

The girls had someone take a group photo of them with the band and then they took single photos of each other with the band.

What really made the evening so enjoyable was seeing people doing *slow summer dancin'* to *rock 'n' roll* music which really did seemed somewhat out of place.

They arrived at the airport and were booked on the *Spirit Of America* Airlines.

"*Let's stick together* on the plane." said Barbara-Ann.

So they asked for their seat allocations to be together Marcy had the window seat, so for most of the fight, she looked out of the window but from a few seats back she was able to listen to *Movies is magic* which was playing on the flight T.V. screen before one of the cabin crew asked them to please use their headphones as the movie was disturbing other passengers.

They seemed to be in the air for so long and then suddenly out of the window Marcy saw the *Sloop John B.* and said "*Land ahoy.*" as she noticed the distant mountains that had a color range from *lavender* to *deep purple* although she knew that they were really greens and browns.

"*This whole world* is so *wonderful*, what with the *sunshine* from that *soulful old man sunshine*, especially *all summer long*, the *moonshine* that tells you *here comes the night*, the *rainbows* in the sky when the sun shines and it rains at the same time and the feeling you get when you *let the wind blow* through your hair." she thought.

As they were coming into land from over the ocean, she saw quite a few males out *surfin'* and then she spotted a *surfer girl*.

"I wonder how many of them would like to go on a *surfin' safari*, go *surfin' U.S.A.*" was the thought that went through her mind at seeing them below her.

Marcy said to Wendy "*Surf's up* down there and I bet you would love to be out in it right now?"

Wendy tried to look out of the window at the surf and said "That would be *wonderful.*"

LANDED

The girls were all excited when the plane taxied into the *Spirit Of America* terminal in *California* and after retrieving all their lugged, they were walking towards the exit to catch the shuttle bus to Koma, when Marcy heard her name being called.

She turned inquisitively to see her father standing there beside her and Brian standing just behind him. Surprised at seeing her father, Marcy turned to Wendy and said excitedly *"He came down*; my father has come all this way just to meet me and Brian too, who was still standing behind him."

Wendy looked at Barbara-Ann and said "That's Brian just behind her dad! *He's a doll.* I'll be his *surfer girl* anytime and he can *meet me in my dreams* tonight and any other night and just *cuddle up* to me. I don't think that I'd be a *baby blue* because he wouldn't be a *run-around lover.*

Lucky Marcy, we'd be the ones *runnin' around the world* to find someone like him."

"Wendy." said Barbara-Ann "Behave yourself, you're *California dreaming* again, yet, he does look like a *dream angel."*

"Kiss me baby" for I'd love to have a *crack at your love* if Marcy's not interested." she thought.

Then she said *"Aren't you glad* that we're with Marcy and meeting her father and Brian."

Marcy introduced the girls to her father then did the *intro* to Brian.

Her father said to her "Brian said last week that *wouldn't it be nice* and a surprise for you if we were here to meet you when you arrived back, so we have done something better.

Although I know that you'll be with your friends, Brian and I have booked into the *Finders Keepers* Trailer Park for two weeks so I can have that well earned holiday and we can get together occasionally and maybe you can show me some of your surfin' moves.

We hired a station wagon so if you girls would like to step this way, we'll get started on our trip home."

The car ride to Koma was a welcomed one as it meant the girls wouldn't have to struggle with their luggage and be sitting down travelling for a longer period of time on the bus.

The trip was full of chatter about where the girls had been and what they had been doing. Wendy and Barbara-Ann were fascinated with Brian, asking him all sorts of questions and his *male ego* was lapping it up.

They finally reached the summer house where the men helped the girls with their luggage. After awhile, Marcy's father said to Brian "Come on it's time to get along and leave these young ladies to settle in and relax. Maybe tomorrow, being Saturday, we might be able to get together again."

Then he said to Marcy "It really is *wonderful* to see you again, baby. You know *I just wasn't made for these times* of being on my own but *I'm so lonely* back at the farm *busy doin' nothin' with all this is that* and my *thoughts of you* always keep me going. I am so glad that Brian comes around, even if it's only because of you.

He has been such a good friend and one day he said to me "*You need a mess of help to stand alone.*" and I believe I do, but I am also happy that *you still believe in me*. I know that for you to have *time to get alone* you have to *breakaway* from home but I also know that *we got love* that other parents and children don't have. You'll never be one of those people who only drop in to see the *old fols at home* when they are passing by."

Then he said "*Oh darlin', let your hair grow long* again. Why did you have to cut it?"

They both laughed and Marcy told her father that she would see him for awhile tomorrow.

The summer house was just a short walk past two cabins and a large shady park to the beach, so after Marcy had finished unpacking, she went for a walk to see the beach and ocean that she had grown to love. The other two girls said that they would join her soon, as they still had a few things to do first.

As Marcy was passing the second cabin, something made her stop and look at the cabin; it felt familiar in some way. There were *wind chimes* hanging down one side that rang in a familiar tune and there was smoke coming from around the back, as if someone was cooking on a campfire.

Then she heard "*Lay down Burden*, it's only Marcella."

The old master painter stepped around the corner and said "*Hey little tomboy, you're welcome* to come in if you want to and spend some time with us. *It's about time* you got here and I'm glad you didn't just *walk on by.*"

Then she heard the *pitter patter* of Burden's feet.

Marcy was so surprised to see the old master painter that she stumbled as she walked in. They sat and talked for awhile about her Hawaiian experience, the friends that she had made; what she was doing there in Koma and many other things including her old school on *Auld Lang Syne* Road and before leaving, she promised to return within a few days for a longer visit.

She was walking out of the drive just as the other two girls were walking past and asked her what was going on and why was she visiting that old man.

Marcy told them about how she had known the old master painter all her life and how her father had told her in one of his letters, about him leaving just after she had left for Hawaii.

Wendy said "That old man has been living here for years and I have never known him to leave, not even have had a holiday."

Then both Barbara Anne and Wendy caught a glimpse of the old painter.

On seeing him Barbara Anne said with a shocked look on her face "Do you know who people say he is? They have always called him Earth Angel, David and they say that *strange things happen* after he has spoken to you, good things, *wonderful* things but strange, and love usually ends up coming into the picture. He can turn up anywhere and at anytime to anyone. Are you sure that he's the same person that you know?"

"Yes. I grew up living on the farm near his cabin and I often visited him. He really is a good artist and friend. I am so glad *we're together again* and I will have to tell dad that he's here." said Marcy as she headed to the beach with the other two girls.

HE'S GONE

It was Saturday morning and the girls slept in and over breakfast they discussed their plans for the day. Wendy said that she was going to hit the beach and if *the surf's up;* she was going to do some *surfin'* and catch up with her beach friends.

Barbara-Ann was going to contact her family and take her little sister out or arrange to meet her some where and Marcy was going to spend most of the day with her father and maybe Brian and also familiarize herself with the town.

Wendy grabbed her board and took off to the beach. Barbara-Ann contacted her father who said that he had just dropped Cindy off at the beach and would stop in on his way home.

Ten minutes later, Barbara-Ann's father was at the house and was asked to stay awhile but he apologized saying *"Sherry, she needs me,* well, *she says she needs me.* You know it's *the same song over and over* again until now it's become a *California saga. Come go with me* back to the beach and find Cindy then we can go home together for a few hours. *I can't wait too long* for you to find your sister, so let's get going."

At the beach Barbara-Ann spotted her sister quickly and called out *"Cindy, oh Cindy."* just as another young girl went to hit her sister. Barbara-Ann rushed towards Cindy shouting *"Caroline, no. Don't hurt my little sister* if she hasn't done anything to you."

As she reached Cindy, Barbara Anne gathered up her sister's belongings and said "Come with me Cindy, dad *can't wait too long* for us to go home with him."

"I'm gonna *getcha back* for getting my part in the school play. *I'm The Pied Piper*, not you." said Caroline.

Cindy replied "I am playing *I'm The Pied Piper* in the band not the play."

"Oh, I'm sorry." said Caroline "I won't have to *getcha back* then if you're not taking my part in the play." and walked away.

Marcy left her house and followed the directions that her father had given her to get to the trailer park, just a mile away.

When she arrived at the park, she met her father coming out of the office where he had just received a message from Brian, saying that his *little deuce coupe* had some sort of engine trouble and that *H.E.L.P. is on the way.*

They walked back to the bungalow arm in arm and Marcy told her father about meeting the old master painter again.

"Are you sure that he is the same man who lived near us and why has he settled here of all places? I thought that he would have been on the other side of the country by now." asked her father.

Marcy replied "I am as surprised as you are by running into him. He said that he was expecting me so how did he know that I was coming here?"

Both Marcy and her father were full of questions so they decided to go and visit him to see if they could get some answers.

When they arrived at the cabin, the old master painter welcomed them by saying "Here, *take a load off your feet.*" as he produced a couple of chairs for them to sit on. The *wind chimes* that had been still suddenly began to ring, even though there wasn't a hint of a breeze from any direction.

The old painter asked Marcy about the time she had spent in Monterey and if she had had a *Funky Pretty* Ding Dang; ice-cream soda, at the *Cabinessence* café.

Then he said "Remember, *always be true to your school* motto and help people in need. You always give *good vibrations* to everyone you meet and *good times* will keep coming if you keep bringing *joy to the world* around you. The *little girl I once knew* is now one of the *California girls*.

The *winds of change* will *wake the world* and *God only knows* what changes will happen. *I get around* and I see, hear and feel what's going on in *this whole world.*

Sometimes, I try to help fix an issue or problem or I try to make a wish or dream come true. *Let the wind blow* in your hair, and the *sunshine* will always shine on you. So *let it shine* in your heart and always *add some music to your day* and you will never go wrong.

Thank you for your kindness *and your dreams come true* if you believe in them and yourself."

Then he turned to her father and said *"The times are a-changin'* for you too. You have been *walkin' the line* for too long now. You have been a good parent and have brought your daughter up to be a good person.

When a man needs a woman in his life to share the burdens with, you tried your best to keep your family together, but the *California role* part was just too much for you in the *games two can play*, so you bowed out gracefully. Don't *hang on to your ego* so tightly anymore, because *happy days* for you are just around the corner.

You have been walking down the *long promised road* all these years and now it's your turn to find *someone to love* and who will love you in return."

As he got up and walked around the side of his cabin, he said *"You've touched me* with the friendship and the *good vibrations* that both of you have given me over the past years. Both of you will spend *one more night alone* but that's all."

They heard a *little bird* tweet, and then saw the *wings of a dove* fly off into the distance. Then all was quiet.

"When the old painter comes back, I will ask him for answers to the questions that we both have. It will be better if the questions come from me and not you because I am older." said her father.

Both Marcy and her father sat there for a short time waiting for the old painter to return, but when he didn't, they both went looking for him and it was Marcy who said "He's Gone.

The cabin is empty. There is only one door here and we didn't see him leave.

His dog is gone too."

SURPRISES

On the way back to the trailer park, Marcy and her father talked about the strange and sudden disappearance of the old painter and what he had said to both of them, especially the last part, where after tonight, neither of them would never be alone again.

It was *good timin'* on their part because they reached the bungalow just as Brian drove up and parked.

He had just gotten out of the car and seemed a little confused "I don't know what's *goin' on* around here." he said "*This car of mine* has never given me trouble before. The mechanic who came to look at it was my cousin *Stevie* and I was so *stoked* at seeing him again after seven years.

We got talking and he offered me a job at his motor vehicle place called *Punchline*. They work on all cars, even custom jobs. If I take the job, I'll have to go *back home* in the next few days to tell my folks and pack a few things to bring back here. I *can't wait too long* to make up my mind."

Marcy said to Brian "Well, that's the sort of job that you've always dreamt of doing, but can't do back home as the town isn't big enough. Now give me *one good reason* for not taking it?"

Brian thought "*She knows me too well.*" then said "I can't think of one. *It's all over* between me and *Lana* so I don't have a thing to keep me there anymore, except for your father. My parents won't mind me leaving especially when they know that I'll be working with Stevie."

They all turned and walked towards the bungalow and a strange feeling overcame Marcy and she stopped suddenly as her father opened the door and walked inside.

There, propped up on the table was a portrait of Marcy when she was about ten years old dressed in a soft blue dress with darker blue ribbon entwined through lace that tied in bows around the neckline and around the short sleeves. The same darker blue ribbon was tied in her hair and a letter propped up to one side of the picture.

Her father said "Where did this come from and how did whoever get into this locked place?"

"Open the letter dad." said Marcy inquisitively, "It might tell you who left it and why."

With trembling hands her father opened the letter and all it said was "This painting of Marcy, I call *Little Girl, You're My Miss America*. I painted it from memory. She is actually an angel but *don't let her know she's an angel. We got love* from her that no-one else will ever have."

When her father read the name of the painting and said it was her, Marcy said "*That's not me*. I never looked that pretty."

Both Brian and her father said in unison "Yes you did, that's how you really looked back then and you're even prettier now."

Marcy looked at the painting again and noticed the letter D in the bottom right hand corner of the painting, but said nothing.

The day seemed so unbelievable and confusing for Marcy. "*All I wanna do* is to go home." she thought so she told her father that it was time for her to go.

He and Brian started walking Marcy home, when a woman called out "*Louie, Louie* Baxter. I thought it was you. How are you?"

Louie turned to see an old high school sweetheart walking towards him from the bungalow next door.

"*Judy*, well I never thought I'd ever see you again. I'm ok, how are you?"

They talked for a few minutes but because both were doing something else at that time, they agreed to catch up later that evening in the restaurant.

Marcy, Louie, Brian, Wendy and Barbara-Ann all arrived at the summer house together and just as they opened the front door, they all heard the wind chimes, that had been placed along the porch beams, without anyone noticing them, ringing out with the *sound of free* energy.

When they walked through the door, there propped up on the hall table was a painting that Marcy immediately recognized and another letter.

Marcy rushed forward and tore open the letter and read out loud "This painting is called *Transcendental Meditation* I know that it was your favorite painting of mine.

If *you still believe in me*, then both the painting and the wind chimes will give you the feel of *endless harmony forever*. Always share your *good vibrations* with everybody wherever you go.

Please tell Wendy that she will go *surfin' U.S.A.* in a car called *Boogie Woodie* and that *forever she'll be my surfer girl*.

Please tell Barbara-Ann that *I know there's an answer* to her *prayer* and *it's just a matter of time* before it gets answered. *God only knows* exactly when and how so *don't back down* too quickly or go *chasin' the sky*. She'll know what I mean."

Marcy looked at the painting again and noticed the letter D in the same place as her father's painting.

Everyone went into the kitchen and made coffee which they took outside to the porch to drink.

Wendy said "I've heard that strange things happen after talking to the old painter, also known as Earth Angel David, but this is either an incredible incident or just a coincidence because I have just met an old friend at the beach, who calls her van Boogie Woodie and she is saving for a surfing trip around the States and said that I would be most welcome to go with her."

With a choked voice and teary eyes, Barbara-Ann said "When I was growing up, we used to visit grandpa a lot and if he caught us day dreaming, he would say "Chasing the sky again, trying to *keep an eye on summer*." He passed away a year after mother got sick."

They all sat quietly for about the next half hour as if everyone was doing some *soul searchin'*. Marcy was still trying to take in all the events that had happened during the day.

It was Brian who broke the silence with "*Wontcha come out tonight* and we'll go and see *Heroes and Villains* playing down at the *Island Fever* Outdoor Club."

Louis declined stating that he had a previous engagement that he wanted to keep and the girls agreed to out with him.

CHANGING LIVES

During the course of the next three months, Brian took the job with his cousin at Punchline and although he learnt a lot more about cars and how to fix them, he has also taught his cousin a lot about customizing vehicles, mainly cars and the business has grown considerably. He still spends a lot of time with Marcy.

One evening Brian said to Marcy "*I just got paid* so will you go out *with me tonight. All summer long* you and the *girls on the beach* have been *keeping summer alive* with your *good vibrations*.

You are not *the little girl I once knew* anymore and *you're so good to me* and for me, to the extent that I want you to *be my baby* permanently. So *let's put our hearts together* and don't *let us go on this way*, just as friends anymore.

I get around a lot more while road testing cars and I have found out that *Heroes and Villains* are playing down at *The Right Lane* Surf Club tonight and we could *dance, dance, dance* for as long as want to."

Louie and Judy became good friends and started going out again. Judy always had the same bungalow when she visited Koma because she was the actual owner of the park. She had bought it just after her husband had died at sea and had a small plaque, with *Sail On Sailor* engraved on it, placed in the small garden outside her bungalow.

Judy's mother, who was known around town as *the little old lady from Pasadena* and her daughters often visited Judy when she came to Koma.

Judy showed Louie a photo of her daughters, that she had hung on the dining room wall, and pointing them out said "This is *my Diane*, the other one is *my Jeanie* and the dog is *Ruby Baby*. I thought that my family would be all I have left *'til I die* until now. Something is telling me that we were meant to meet up again."

One afternoon, Louie said to Marcella, "*Darlin'*, as you are aware I have been taking Judy out and the other night, I found out that *love is a woman* who you can relate to and who gives you *good vibrations* in return.

God only knows what's *goin' on* between Judy and me, but the other night when we were out I said "*Let's do it again, do you wanna dance*? I didn't understand as to *how could we still be dancin'* to *the same song* like we did when we were in high school and *our sweet love* has seemed to be re-kindled; *then I kissed* her under *the surfer moon.*

I will love your mother *'til I die* and Judy, well, *she knows me too well* to *hurry love* but *I wanna be around* her because *she believes in love again* and I know that I can give it to her.

Just after we graduated her folks took her on an overseas holiday but she returned home engaged so I started travelling and met your mother. I never thought that after all these years; I could get *the one you can't have* from my school days."

Louie got the *California feeling* and heard *California calling* so he went back to the cotton fields and sold the farm to Caroline. "*Caroline, no*, I never thought that I would be *leaving this town.*" he said as he handed her the property keys, before driving back to California and his new life with Judy who had moved into the Trailer Park permanently after renting out her other house.

Wendy finished her three months of the work exchange program at the place *Trader* had arranged for her. She had learnt the *surfer's rule* and how to stop a *surf jam* when she was out *surfin'*. She became an instructor and taught her students how to *catch a wave* when the *surf's up.*

"This is the *one for the boys* to ride in because they will all want to try and make it and will crowd the wave." she said to the only *surfer girl* that she was teaching in this class.

Wendy's friend, Deirdre was also an excellent *surfer girl* who was able to *slip on through* any size wave when the *surf's up.*

When it was *night time*, Wendy became a *rocking surfer* because the *spirit of rock 'n' roll* was in her heart as well as surfing. She would often say "*I'm waiting for the day* that I'll be *still cruisin'* and *still surfin'* when the *surf's up* all around the States."

Wendy and Deirdre made plans to leave at the end of the year to go *surfin' U.S.A.*

"*Wouldn't it be nice* if *your summer dream* could come true under *that lucky old sun* who will always *keep an eye on summer* and you?" Marcy said to her one day.

After her work program finished, Barbara-Ann became a production assistant at *Pet Sounds* Recording Studio and also became very good friends with the band *Heroes and Villains*.

Whenever *Youngblood* (Andy) from the band *Heroes and Villains* was in town, he and Barbara-Ann would spend time together.

One night when the band was in town and Andy had the evening off Barbara-Ann said "*Shut Down* has come to town and since *I just got my pay*, let's all go and see it again while we all have the chance.

While Barbara-Ann went to get the tickets, Andy said to Marcy "*I get around* and I see and meet many people but *there's no other* person that I want to be with except for Barbara-Ann. *She's got rhythm* and *we gotta groove* happening but I won't be happy until *she's mine.*

Here she comes, please don't say anything to her until I can find a way to tell her myself?"

After the show, it was *rock and roll to the rescue* and *fun, fun, fun.*

Barbara-Ann's mother was admitted to hospital for an emergency operation to cure her illness. Barbara-Ann's father said to her reassuringly "*Don't worry baby*, your mother will be fine and will be home soon."

In fact six weeks later, her mother was home and doing very well on her road to recovery from the surgery to remove a brain tumor that had just been diagnosed.

Marcy, however, finished her work exchange program at the radio station, then left to become a support worker in a community organization.

One day on her way home, she saw the old master painter at the cabin where he was living before and he called out to her "Marcella, *you are my sunshine.*" and then disappeared around the corner.

Marcy ran to find him but like once before he had disappeared completely.

That evening when she told Wendy about seeing the old painter again and what he had said to her.

Wendy said "That's your *imagination* playing tricks on you. You told me yourself that he had disappeared into thin air when you and your father had visited him."

Marcy said to Wendy "Sometimes when I'm *in my room* I get this strange feeling that makes me want to look *at my window* and then I hear the wind chimes.

In the back of my mind, I hear the old painter saying, "Always *be true to your school* motto because you have a *good kind of love* and *good vibrations* that the world needs."

Those nights, after *I went to sleep*, I would dream of Denny and wonder how my mother could *let him run wild* as they were living so close to the river.

The following day, I would wake with *tears in the morning* and think that even though *I'm so young, I'm in great shape, it's ok* to feel like I do. Because *it's a beautiful day*, don't get caught up in the *summertime blues*. Just *live let live*, here today and don't start *looking at tomorrow*."

I know *the shift* from the country to California has changed Brian's life, my father's life and my life in so many *wonderful* ways that it all seems like a dream but this has been a *summer of love* for some people and for others where *summer means new love* for them.

Please let me wonder forever if the old master painter was really the person you said he was, because *paradise found* me here in California and I still believe in him."

The last words in this story come from the old master painter "*Why do fools fall in love*?

Well, it's because they are not fools at the time it happens.

If *you still believe in me, make a wish* and it may very well come true or pray and ask God to hear *our prayer* for *I know there's an answer* that will be forth coming when you least expect it.

What more can I say; except to *add some music* to your day and believe in yourself, for you can achieve anything you want to do or be. *Wouldn't it be nice* to be able to say "I have done what I set out to do or be?"

Share some of your love and you will get love in return.

Am I Earth Angel, David?

Well, I'm not going to tell you because *I get around* everywhere to *save the day* for many people who really need me.

Always remember to just live your life the best way that you can and never give up hope and never try to be the person you are not. You are unique and special in your own way.

Go on… keep smiling and have lots of fun".

REFERENCE

SUMMER DAYS (AND SUMMER NIGHTS)
THE GIRL FROM NEW YORK CITY
AMUSEMENT PARKS U.S.A.
THEN I KISSED HER
SALT LAKE CITY
GIRL DON'T TELL ME
HELP ME, RHONDA
CALIFORNIA GIRLS
LET HIM RUN WILD
YOU'RE SO GOOD TO ME
SUMMER MEANS NEW LOVE
I'M BUGGER AT MY OL' MAN
AND YOUR DREAM COMES TRUE

ULTIMATE CHRISTMAS
LITTLE SAINT NICK (SINGLE VERSION)
AULD LANG SYNE (ALTERNATE MIX)
LITTLE SAINT NICK (ALTERNATE MIX)
CHILD OF WINTER
SANTA'S GOT AN AIRPLANE
CHRISTMAS TIME IS HERE AGAIN
WINTER SYMPHONY
(I SAW SANTA) ROCKIN' AROUND THE CHRISTMAS TREE
MELEKALIKIMAKA
BELLS OF CHRISTMAS
MORNING CHRISTMAS
TOY DRIVE PUBLIC SERVICE ANNOUNCEMENT
DENIS WILSON CHRISTMAS MESSAGE
BRIAN WILSON CHRISTMAS INTERVIEW

CHRISTMAS ALBUM
LITTLE SAINT NICK
THE MAN WITH ALL THE TOYS
SANTA'S BEARD
MERRY CHRISTMAS BABY
CHRISTMAS DAY
FROSTY THE SNOWMAN
WE THREE KINGS OF ORIENT ARE
BLUE CHRISTMAS
SANTA CLAUS IS COMING TO TOWN
WHITE CHRISTMAS

I'LL BE HOME FOR CHRISTMAS
AULD LANG SYNE

CONCERT
FUN, FUN, FUN
THE LITTLE OLD LADY FROM PASADENA
LITTLE DEUCE COUPE
LONG TALL TEXAN
IN MY ROOM
MONSTER MASH
LET'S GO TRIPPIN'
PAPA-OOM-MOW-MOW
THE WANDERER
HAWAII
GRADUATION DAY
I GET AROUND
JOHNNY B. GOODE

ALL SUMMER LONG
I GET AROUND
ALL SUMMER LONG
HUSHABYE
LITTLE HONDA
WE'LL RUN AWAY
CARL'S BIG CHANCE
WENDY
DO YOU REMEMBER
GIRLS ON THE BEACH
DRIVE-IN
OUR FAVORITE RECORDING SESSIONS
DON'T BACK DOWN

SHUT DOWN VOLUME 2
FUN, FUN, FUN
DON'T WORRY BABY
IN THE PARKIN' LOT
'CASSIUS' LOVE vs. 'SONNY' WILSON
THE WARMTH OF THE SUN
THIS CAR OF MINE
WHY DO FOOLS FALL IN LOVE
POM POM PLAY GIRL
KEEP AN EYE ON SUMMER
SHUT DOWN PART II

LOUIE LOUIE
DENNY'S DRUMS

FRIENDS
WAKE THE WORLD
BE HERE IN THE MORNING
WHEN A MAN NEEDS A WOMAN
PASSING BY
ANNA LEE, THE HEALER
LITTLE BIRD
BE STILL
BUSY DOIN' NOTHIN'
DIAMOND HEAD
TRANSCENDENTAL MEDITATION

WILD HONEY
WILD HONEY
AREN'T YOU GLAD
I WAS MADE TO LOVE HER
COUNTRY AIR
A THING OR TWO
DARLIN'
I'D LOVE JUST ONCE TO SEE YOU
HERE COMES THE NIGHT
LET THE WIND BLOW
HOW SHE BOOGALOOED IT
MAMA SAYS

SMILEY SMILE
HEROES AND VILLAINS
VEGETABLES
FALL BREAKS AND BACK TO WINTER
SHE'S GOIN BALD
LITTLE PAD
GOOD VIBRATIONS
WITH ME TONIGHT
WIND CHIMES
GETTING' HUNGRY
WONDERFUL
WHISTLE IN

PET SOUNDS
WOULDN'T IT BE NICE
YOU STILL BELIEVE IN ME

46

THAT'S NOT ME
DON'T TALK (PUT YOUR HEAD ON MY SHOULDER)
I'M WAITING FOR THE DAY
LET'S GO AWAY FOR AWHILE
SLOOP JOHN B
GOD ONLY KNOWS
I KNOW THERE'S AN ANSWER
HERE TODAY
I JUST WASN'T MADE FOR THESE TIMES
PET SOUNDS
CAROLINE, NO

RECORDED "LIVE" AT A BEACH BOYS' PARTY!
HULLY GULLY
I SHOULD HAVE KNOWN BETTER
TELL ME WHY
PAPA-OOM-MOW-MOW
MOUNTAIN OF LOVE
YOU'VE GOT TO HIDE YOUR LOVE AWAY
DEVOTED TO YOU
ALLEY OOP
THERE'S NO OTHER (LIKE MY BABY)
MEDLEY: I GET AROUND/LITTLE DEUCE COUPE
THE TIMES THEY ARE A-CHANGIN'
BARBARA ANN

TODAY
DO YOU WANNA DANCE
GOOD TO MY BABY
DON'T HURT MY LITTLE SISTER
WHEN I GROW UP (TO BE A MAN)
HELP ME, RHONDA
DANCE, DANCE, DANCE
PLEASE LET ME WONDER
I'M SO YOUNG
KISS ME BABY
SHE KNOWS ME TOO WELL
IN THE BACK OF MY MIND
BULL SESSION WITH BIG DADDY

LOOKING BACK WITH LOVE
LOOKING BACK WITH LOVE
ON AND ON AND ON
RUNNIN' AROUND THE WORLD

OVER AND OVER
ROCKIN' THE MAN IN THE BOAT
CALENDAR GIRL
BE MY BABY
ONE GOOD REASON
TEACH ME TONIGHT
PARADISE FOUND

PACIFIC OCEAN BLUE
RIVER SONG
WHAT'S WRONG
MOONSHINE
FRIDAY NIGHT
DREAMER
THOUGHTS OF YOU
TIME
YOU AND I
PACIFIC OCEAN BLUES
FAREWELL MY FRIEND
RAINBOWS
END OF THE SHOW

YOUNGBLOOD (CARL WILSON)
WHAT MORE CAN I SAY
SHE'S MINE
GIVIN' YOU UP
ONE MORE NIGHT ALONE
ROCKIN' ALL OVER THE WORLD
WHAT DO YOU WANT
YOUNGBLOOD
OF THE TIMES
TOO EARLY TOO TELL
IF I COULD TALK TO LOVE
TIME
LIKE A BROTHER

TODAY
I WISH FOR YOU
RUN DON'T WALK
THEY'RE ONLY WORDS
LIKE A BROTHER

CARL WILSON
HOLD ON
BRIGHT LIGHTS
WHAT YOU GONNA DO ABOUT ME
THE RIGHT LANE
HURRY LOVE
HEAVEN
THE GRAMMY
SEEMS SO LONG AGO

MISCELLANEOUS BRIAN WILSON TRACKS
THIS SONG WANTS TO SLEEP WITH YOU TONIGHT
ON CHRISTMAS DAY
SILENT NIGHT
JOY TO THE WORLD
HE COULDN'T GET HIS POOR BODY TO MOVE
BEING WITH THE ONE YOU LOVE
LET'S GO TO HEAVEN IN MY CAR
TOO MUCH SUGAR
WALKING DOWN THE PATH OF LIFE/LOVE AND MERCY
WHAT LOVE CAN DO
BELIEVE IN YOURSELF
LIVE LET LIVE

THAT LUCKY OLD SUN (BRIAN WILSON)
THAT LUCKY OLD SUN
MORNING BEAT
NARRATIVE: ROOM WITH A VIEW
GOOD KIND OF LOVE
FOREVER SHE'LL BE MY SURFER GIRL
NARRATIVE: VENICE BEACH
LIVE LET LIVE/THAT LUCKY OLE SUN (REPRISE)
MEXICAN GIRL
NARRATIVE: CINCO DE MAYO
CALIFORNIA ROLE/THAT LUCKY OLD SUN (REPRISE)
NARRATIVE: BETWEEN PICTURES
OXYGEN TO THE BRAIN
CAN'T WAIT TOO LONG
MIDNIGHT'S ANOTHER DAY
THAT LUCKY OLD SUN (REPRISE)
GOING HOME
SOUTHERN CALIFORNIA

WHAT I REALLY WANT FOR CHRISTMAS
(BRIAN WILSON)
THE MAN WITH ALL THE TOYS
WHAT I REALLY WANT FOR CHRISTMAS
GOD REST YOU MERRY GENTLEMEN
O HOLY NIGHT
WE WISH YOU A MERRY CHRISTMAS
HARK THE HERALD ANGELS SING
IT CAME UPON A MIDNIGHT CLEAR
THE FIRST NOEL
CHRISTMASEY
LITTLE SAINT NICK
DECK THE HALLS
AULD LANG SYNE

SMiLE (BRIAN WILSON)
OUR PRAYER/GEE
HEROES AND VILLAINS
ROLL PLYMOUTH ROCK
BARNYARD
OLD MASTER PAINTER/YOU ARE MY SUNSHINE
CABIN ESSENCE
WONDERFUL
SONG FOR CHILDREN
CHILD IS THE FATHER OF THE MAN
SURF'S UP
I'M IN GREAT SHAPE/I WANNA BE AROUND/WORKSHOP
VEGA-TABLES
ON A HOLIDAY
WIND CHIMES
MRS O'LEARY'S COW
IN BLUE HAWAII
GOOD VIBRATIONS

GETTING' IN OVER MY HEAD
(BRIAN WILSON)
HOW COULD WE BE STILL DANCIN'
SOUL SEARCHIN'
YOU'VE TOUCHED ME
GETTING' IN OVER MY HEAD
CITY BLUES
DESERT DRIVE
A FRIEND LIKE YOU

50

MAKE A WISH
RAINBOW EYES
SATURDAY MORNING IN THE CITY
FAIRY TALE
DON'T LET HER KNOW SHE'S AN ANGEL
THE WALTZ

BRIAN WILSON PRESENTS PET SOUNDS LIVE
SHOW INTRO
WOULDN'T IT BE NICE
YOU STILL BELIEVE IN ME
THAT'S NOT ME
DON'T TALK (PUT YOUR HEAD ON MY SHOULDER)
I'M WAITING FOR THE DAY
LET'S GO AWAY FOR AWHILE
SLOOP JOHN B
GOD ONLY KNOWS
I KNOW THERE'S AN ANSWER
HERE TODAY
I JUST WASN'T MADE FOR THESE TIMES
PET SOUNDS
CAROLINE, NO

LIVE AT THE ROXY
BAND INTRO
BRIAN WILSON
'TIL I DIE
DARLIN'
LET'S GO AWAY FOR AWILE
PET SOUNDS
GOD ONLY KNOWS
LAY DOWN BURDEN
BE MY BABY
GOOD VIBRATIONS
CAROLINE, NO
ALL SUMMER LONG
LOVE AND MERCY

LITTLE DEUCE COUPE
LITTLE DEUCE COUPE
BALLAD OF OLE' BETSY
BE TRUE TO YOUR SCHOOL
CAR CRAZY CUTIE

CHERRY CHERRY COUPE
409
SHUT DOWN
SPIRIT OF AMERICA
OUR CAR CLUB
NO-GO SHOWBOAT
A YOUNG MAN IS GONE
CUSTOM MACHINE

SURFER GIRL
SURFER GIRL
CATCH A WAVE
THE SURFER MOON
SOUTH BAY SURFER
ROCKING SURFER
LITTLE DEUCE COUPE
IN MY ROOM
HAWAII
SURFER'S RULE
OUR CAR CLUB
YOUR SUMMER DREAM
BOOGIE WOODIE

SURFIN' U.S.A.
SURFIN' U.S.A.
FARMER'S DAUGHTER
MISIRLOU
STOKED
LONELY SEA
SHUT DOWN
NOBLE SURFER
HONKY TONK
LANA
SURF JAM
LET'S GO TRIPPIN'
FINDERS KEEPERS

SURFIN' SAFARI
SURFIN' SAFARI
COUNTY FAIR
TEN LITTLE INDIANS
CHUG-A-LUG
LITTLE GIRL (YOU'RE MY MISS AMERICA)

409
SURFIN'
HEADS YOU WIN, TAILS I LOSE
SUMMERTIME BLUES
CUCKOO CLOCK
MOON DAWG
THE SHIFT

LIVE AT THE ROXY (BRIAN WILSON)
LITTLE GIRL INTRO
THE LITTLE GIRL I ONCE KNEW
THIS WHOLE WORLD
DON'T WORRY BABY
KISS ME BABY
DO IT AGAIN
CALIFORNIA GIRLS
I GET AROUND
BACK HOME
IN MY ROOM
SURFER GIRL
THE FIRST TIME
THIS ISN'T LOVE
ADD SOME MUSIC TO YOUR DAY
PLEASE LET ME WONDER

THE WILSONS
(CARNIE AND WENDY WILSON)
MONDAY WITHOUT YOU
MIRACLE
'TIL I DIE
EVERYTHING I NEED

IMAGINATION (BRIAN WILSON)
YOUR IMAGINATION
SHE SAYS SHE NEEDS ME
SOUTH AMERICAN
WHERE HAVE YOU BEEN?
KEEP AN EYE ON SUMMER
DREAM ANGEL
CRY
LAY DOWN BURDEN
LET HIM RUN WILD
SUNSHINE
HAPPY DAYS

53

ORANGE CRATE ART
VAN DYKE PARKS WITH BRIAN WILSON
ORANGE CRATE ART
SAIL AWAY
MY HOBO HEART
WINGS OF A DOVE
PALM TREE AND MOON
SUMMER IN MONTEREY
SAN FRANCISCO
HOLD BACK TIME
MY JEANINE
MOVIES IS MAGIC
THIS TOWN GOES DOWN AT SUNSET
LULLABYE

I JUST WASN'T MADE FOR THESE TIMES
(BRIAN WILSON)
MEANT FOR YOU
THIS WHOLE WORLD
CAROLINE, NO
LET THE WIND BLOW
LOVE AND MERCY
DO IT AGAIN
THE WARMTH OF THE SUN
WONDERFUL
STILL I DREAM OF IT
MELT AWAY
'TIL I DIE

BRIAN WILSON
LOVE AND MERCY
WALKIN' THE LINE
MELT AWAY
BABY LET YOUR HAIR GROW LONG
LITTLE CHILDREN
ONE FOR THE BOYS
THERE'S SO MANY
NIGHT TIME
LET IT SHINE
MEET ME IN MY DREAMS
RIO GRANDE

SUMMER IN PARADISE
HOT FUN IN THE SUMMERTIME
SURFIN'
SUMMER OF LOVE
ISLAND FEVER
STILL SURFIN'
SLOW SUMMER DANCIN' (ONE SUMMER NIGHT)
STRANGE THINGS HAPPEN
REMEMBER "WALKING IN THE SAND"
LAHAINA ALOHA
UNDER THE BOARDWALK
SUMMER IN PARADISE
FOREVER

STILL CRUISIN'
STILL CRUISIN'
SOMEWHERE NEAR JAPAN
ISLAND GIRL (I'M GONNA MAKE HER MINE)
IN MY CAR
KOKOMO
WIPE OUT
MAKE IT BIG
I GET AROUND
WOULDN'T IT BE NICE
CALAFORNIA GIRLS

BEACH BOYS (1985)
GETCHA BACK
IT'S GETTING' LATE
CRACK AT YOUR LOVE
MAYBE I DON'T KNOW
SHE BELIEVES IN LOVE AGAIN
CALIFORNIA CALLING
PASSING FRIEND
I'M SO LONELY
WHERE I BELONG
I DO LOVE YOU
IT'S JUST A MATTER OF TIME
MALE EGO

KEEPIN' THE SUMMER ALIVE
KEEPIN' THE SUMMER ALIVE
OH DARLIN'

SOME OF YOUR LOVE
LIVIN' WITH A HEARTACHE
SCHOOL DAY (RING! RING! GOES THE BELL)
GOIN' ON
SUNSHINE
WHEN GIRLS GET TOGETHER
SANTA ANA WINDS
ENDLESS HARMONY

L.A. (LIGHT ALBUM)
GOOD TIMIN'
LADY LYNDA
FULL SAIL
ANGEL COME HOME
LOVE SURROUNDS ME
SUMAHAMA
HERE COMES THE NIGHT
BABY BLUE
GOIN' SOUTH
SHORTENIN' BREAD

M.I.U. ALBUM
SHE'S GOT RHYTHM
COME GO WITH ME
HEY LITTLE TOMBOY
KONA COAST
PEGGY SUE
WONTCHA COME OUT TONIGHT
SWEET SUNDAY KINDA LOVE
BELLES OF PARIS
PITTER PATTER
MY DIANE
MATCHPOINT OF OUR LOVE
WINDS OF CHANGE

THE BEACH BOYS LOVE YOU
LET US GO ON THIS WAY
ROLLER SKATING CHILD
MONA
JOHNNY CARSON
GOOD TIME
HONKIN' DOWN THE HIGHWAY
DING DANG

SOLAR SYSTEM
THE NIGHT WAS SO YOUNG
I'LL BET HE'S NICE
LET'S PUT OUR HEARTS TOGETHER
I WANNA PICK YOU UP
AIRPLANE
LOVE IS A WOMAN

15 BIG ONES
ROCK 'n' ROLL MUSIC
IT'S OK
HAD TO PHONE YA
CHAPEL OF LOVE
EVERYONE'S IN LOVE WITH YOU
MEDLEY: TALK TO ME/TALLAHASSEE LASSIE
THAT SAME SONG
TM SONG
PALISADE PARK
SUSIE CINCINNATI
A CASUAL LOOK
BLUEBERRY HILL
BACK HOME
IN THE STILL OF THE NIGHT (I'LL REMEMBER)
JUST ONCE IN MY LIFE

IN CONCERT (1972-73)
"SAIL ON SAILOR"
"SLOOP JOHN B"
"TRADER"
"YOU STILL BELIEVE IN ME"
"CALAFORNIA GIRLS"
"DARLIN'"
"MARCELLA"
"CAROLINE, NO"
"LEAVING THIS TOWN"
"HEROES AND VILLAINS"
"FUNKY PRETTY" *** UNFINISHED
"LET THE WIND BLOW"
"HELP ME RHONDA" *** UNFINISHED
"SURFER GIRL"
"WOULDN'T IT BE NICE"
"WE GOT LOVE"
"DON'T WORRY BABY"

57

"SURFIN' U.S.A." *** UNFINISHED
"GOOD VIBRATIONS" *** UNFINISHED
"FUN, FUN, FUN" *** UNFINISHED

MOUNT VERNON AND FAIRWAY
MOUNT VERNON AND FAIRWAY- THEME
I'M THE PIED PIPER- INSTUMENTAL
BETTER GET BACK IN BED
MAGIC TRANSISTOR RADIO
RADIO KING DOM
I'M THE PIED PIPER

HOLLAND
SAIL ON SAILOR
STEAMBOAT
CALIFORNIA SAGA/BIG SUR
CALIFORNIA SAGA/THE BEAKS OF EAGLES
CALIFORNIA SAGA/CALIFORNIA
TRADER
LEAVING THIS TOWN
ONLY WITH YOU
FUNKY PRETTY
MOUNT VERNON AND FAIRWAY LYRICS

CARL AND THE PASSIONS-SO TOUGH
YOU NEED A MESS OF HELP TO STAND ALONE
HERE SHE COMES
HE CAME DOWN
MARCELLA
HOLD ON DEAR BROTHER
MAKE IT GOOD
ALL THIS IS THAT
CUDDLE UP

SURF'S UP
DON'T GO NEAR THE WATER
LONG PROMISED ROAD
TAKE A LOAD OFF YOUR FEET
DISNEY GIRLS
STUDENT DEMONSTRATION TIME
FEEL FLOWS
LOOKING AT TOMORROW
A DAY IN THE LIFE OF A TREE

'TIL I DIE
SURF'S UP

SUNFLOWER
SLIP ON THROUGH
THIS WHOLE WORLD
ADD SOME MUSIC
GOT TO KNOW THE WOMAN
DEIRDRE
IT'S ABOUT TIME
TEARS IN THE MORNING
ALL I WANNA DO
FOREVER
OUR SWEET LOVE
AT MY WINDOW
COOL, COOL WATER

SURFIN' SAFARI/SURFIN' U.S.A.
CINDY, OH CINDY
THE BAKER MAN
LAND AHOY

MISCELLANEOUS BEACH BOYS TRACKS
PROBLEM CHILD
IT'S A BEAUTIFUL DAY
CALIFORNIA DREAMING
SOULFUL OLD MAN SUNSHINE
CHASIN' THE SKY
WE GOT LOVE
JUDY
THE LORD'S PRAYER
ROCK AND ROLL TO THE RESCUE
SEASONS IN THE SUN
THE MONKEY'S UNCLE
OKIE FROM MUSKOGEE
LAVENDER

SPRING
(MARILYN WILSON AND DIANE ROVELL)
THINKIN' 'BOUT YOU BABY
SWEET MOUNTAIN

**PET PROJECTS: THE BRIAN
WILSON PRODUCTIONS**
RUN-AROUND LOVER
THINKIN' 'BOUT YOU BABY
PAMELA JEAN
AFTER THE GAME
THE ONE YOU CAN'T HAVE
GUESS I'M DUMB
HE'S A DOLL

LITTLE DEUCE COUPE/ALL SUMMER LONG
BE TRUE TO YOUR SCHOOL
ALL DRESSED UP FOR SCHOOL
LITTLE HONDA
DON'T BACK DOWN
TODAY/SUMMER DAYS (AND SUMMER NIGHTS!!!)
THE LITTLE GIRL I ONCE KNEW
DANCE, DANCE, DANCE
I'M SO YOUNG
LET HIM RUN WILD
GRADUATION DAY

BONUS TRACKS 1962-1965 FROM CAPITOL "TWOFERS

SURFER/GIRL/SHUT DOWN VOL.2
FUN, FUN, FUN
GANZ ALLEIN (IN MY ROOM)
I DO

**BONUS TRACKS 1966-1969 FROM CAPITOL "TWOFERS"
PET SOUNDS**
UNRELAESED BACKGROUNDS
HANG ON TO YOUR EGO
TROMBONE DIXIE

SMILEY SMILE/WILD HONEY
HEROES AND VILLAINS
GOOD VIBRATIONS (VARIOUS SESSIONS)
GOOD VIBRATIONS (EARLY TAKE)
YOU'RE WELCOME
THEIR HEARTS WERE FULL OF SPRING
CAN'T WAIT TOO LONG

FRIENDS/20-20
BREAKAWAY
CELEBRATE THE NEWS
WE'RE TOGETHER AGAIN
WALK ON BY
OLD FOLS AT HOME/OL' MAN RIVER

20/20
DO IT AGAIN
I CAN HEAR MUSIC
BLUEBIRDS OVER THE MOUNTAIN
BE WITH ME
ALL I WANT TO DO
THE NEAREST FARAWAY PLACE
COTTON FIELDS (COTTON SONG)
I WENT TO SLEEP
TIME TO GET ALONE
NEVER LEARN NOT TO LOVE
OUR PRAYER
CABINESSENCE

SWEET INSANITY (BRIAN WILSON)
INTRO
SOMEONE TO LOVE
WATER BUILDS UP
DON'T LET HER KNOW SHE'S AN ANGEL
DO YOU HAVE ANY REGRETS?
BRIAN
HOTTER
SPIRIT OF ROCK 'N' ROLL
RAINBOW EYES
LOVE YA
MAKE A WISH
SMART GIRLS
COUNTRY FEELIN'
LET'S STICK TOGETHER
CONCERT TONIGHT
SAVE THE DAY
LET'S DO IT AGAIN

**GOOD VIBRATIONS: THIRTY YEARS OF
THE BEACH BOYS
DISC 1**
SURFIN' U.S.A. (DEMO)
LITTLE SURFER GIRL
SURFIN' (REHEARSAL)
SURFIN'
THEIR HEARTS WERE FULL OF SPRING (DEMO)
SURFIN' SAFARI
409
PUNCHLINE
SURFIN' U.S.A.
SHUT DOWN
SURFER GIRL
LITTLE DEUCE COUPE
IN MY ROOM
CATCH A WAVE
THE SURFER MOON
BE TRUE TO YOUR SCHOOL
SPIRIT OF AMERICA
LITTLE SAINT NICK
THINGS WE DID LAST SUMMER
FUN, FUN, FUN
DON'T WORRY BABY
WHY DO FOOLS FALL IN LOVE
THE WARMTH OF THE SUN
I GET AROUND
ALL SUMMER LONG
LITTLE HONDA
WENDY
DON'T BACK DOWN
DO YOU WANNA DANCE
WHEN I GROW UP (TO BE A MAN)
DANCE, DANCE, DANCE
PLEASE LET ME WONDER
SHE KNOWS ME TOO WELL
RADIO STATION JINGLES
CONCERT PROMO/HUSHABYE

GOOD VIBRATIONS: THIRTY YEARS OF
THE BEACH BOYS
DISC 2
CALIFORNIA GIRLS
HELP ME, RHONDA
THEN I KISSED HER
AND YOUR DREAMS COME TRUE
THE LITTLE GIRL I ONCE KNEW
BARBARA ANN
RUBY BABY
KOMA
SLOOP JOHN B
WOULDN'T IT BE NICE
YOU STILL BELIEVE IN ME
GOD ONLY KNOWS
HANG ON TO YOUR EGO
I JUST WASN'T MADE FOR THESE TIMES
PET SOUNDS
CAROLINE, NO
GOOD VIBRATIONS
OUR PRAYER
HEROES AND VILLAINS
HEROES AND VILLAINS (SECTIONS)
WONDERFUL
CABINESSENCE
WIND CHIMES
HEROES AND VILLIANS (INTRO)
DO YOU LIKE WORMS
VEGATABLES
I LOVE TO SAY DA DA
SURF'S UP
WITH ME TONIGHT

GOOD VIBRATIONS: THIRTY YEARS OF
THE BEACH BOYS
DISC 3
HEROES AND VILLAINS
DARLIN'
WILD HONEY
LET THE WIND BLOW
CAN'T WAIT TOO LONG
COOL, COOL WATER
MEANT FOR YOU

FRIENDS
LITTLE BIRD
BUSY DOIN' NOTHIN'
DO IT AGAIN
I CAN HEAR MUSIC
I WENT TO SLEEP
TIME TO GET ALONE
BREAKAWAY
COTTON FIELDS (THE COTTON SONG)
SAN MIGUEL
GAMES TWO CAN PLAY
I JUST GOT MY PAY
THIS WHOLE WORLD
ADD SOME MUSIC
FOREVER
OUR SWEET LOVE
H.E.L.P. IS ON THE WAY
4TH OF JULY
LONG PROMISED ROAD
DISNEY GIRLS
SURF'S UP
'TIL I DIE

**GOOD VIBRATIONS: THIRTY YEARS OF
THE BEACH BOYS
DISC 4**
SAIL ON SAILOR
CALIFORNIA
TRADER
FUNKY PRETTY
FAIRY TALE MUSIC
YOU NEED A MESS OF HELP TO STAND ALONE
MARCELLA
ALL THIS IS THAT
ROCK AND ROLL MUSIC
IT'S OK
HAD TO PHONE YA
THAT SAME SONG
IT'S OVER NOW
STILL I DREAM OF IT
LET US GO ON THIS WAY
THE NIGHT WAS SO YOUNG
I'LL BET HE'S NICE

64

AIRPLANE
COME GO WITH ME
OUR TEAM
BABY BLUE
GOOD TIMIN'
GOIN' ON
GETCHA BACK
KOKOMO

BOX SET BONUS DISC
IN MY ROOM
RADIO SPOT #1 (NOT USED IN STORY)
I GET AROUND (TRACK ONLY)
RADIO SPOT #2 (NOT USED IN STORY)
DANCE, DANCE, DANCE (TRACKING SESSION)
HANG ON TO YOUR EGO (SESSION)
GOD ONLY KNOWS (TRACKING SESSION)
GOOD VIBRATIONS (SESSION)
HEROES AND VILLAINS (TRACK ONLY)
CABINESSENCE (TRACK ONLY)
SURF'S UP (TRACK ONLY)
RADIO SPOT #3 (NOT USED IN STORY)
ALL SUMMER LONG (VOCALS)
WENDY (VOCALS)
HUSHABYE (VOCALS)
WHEN I GROW UP TO BE A MAN (VOCALS)
WOULDN'T IT BE NICE (VOCALS)
CALIFORNIA GIRLS (VOCALS)
RADIO SPOT #4 (NOT USED IN STORY)
CONCERT INTRO/ SURFIN' U.S.A. – LIVE 1964
SURFER GIRL – LIVE 1964
BE TRUE TO YOUR SCHOOL – LIVE 1964
GOOD VIBRATIONS – LIVE 1966
SURFER GIRL – LIVE IN HAWAII REHEARSALS – 1967

**THE SIXTIES...THE SEVENTIES, EIGHTIES,
AND NINETIES OTHER BEACH BOYS...BRIAN
WILSON SOLO ALBUMS AND PROJECTS...
OTHER SOLO ALBUMS...UNRELEASED ALBUMS**

HAWTHORNE HOT SHOTS
"TILL I DIE"
"SAN MIGUEL"
"HEROES AND VILLAINS"

"I JUST GOT MY PAY"
"KAREN"
"GOOD VIBRATIONS"
"LADY"
"MELODY"
"SOUND OF FREE"

CALIFORNIA FEELING
"CALIFORNIA FEELING"
"BRIAN'S BACK"
"OUR TEAM"
"HOW'S ABOUT A LITTLE BIT OF YOUR SWEET LOVIN'"
"I'M BEGGIN' YOU PLEASE"
"SANTA ANA WINDS"
"LOOKIN' DOWN THE COAST"
"LAZY LIZZY"
"CALIFORNIA DREAMING"
"SKATETOWN U.S.A."
"SHERRY, SHE NEEDS ME"
"RIVER SONG"
"STEVIE"
"MARILYN ROVELL"
"WE GOTTA GROOVE"
"CARRY ME HOME"

ADULT CHILD
"LIFE IS FOR THE LIVING"
"HEY LITTLE TOMBOY"
"DEEP PURPLE"
"IT'S OVER NOW"
"EVERYBODY WANTS TO LIVE"
"SHORTNIN' BREAD"
"LINES"
"ON BROADWAY"
"GAMES TWO CAN PLAY"
"IT'S TRYING TO SAY"
"STILL I DREAM OF IT"

LANDLOCKED
"LOOP DE LOOP"
"SUSIE CINCINNATI"
"SAN MIGUEL"
"H.E.L.P. IS ON THE WAY"

"TAKE A LOAD OFF YOUR FEET"
"OVER THE WAVES (CARNIVAL)"
(INSTUMENTAL WITH LA-LAS)
"I JUST GOT PAID"
"IT'S ABOUT TIME"
"TEARS IN THE MORNING"
"GOOD TIMES"
"BIG SUR"
"WHEN GIRLS GET TOGETHER"
"LOOKIN' AT TOMORROW"
"'TIL I DIE"

SMILE
"PRAYER"
"HEROES AND VILLAINS"
"BARNYARD"
"DO YOU LIKE WORMS"
"THE OLD MASTER PAINTER"
"WONDERFUL"
"CHILD IS FATHER OF THE MAN"
"CABINESSENCE"
"GOOD VIBRATIONS"
"WIND CHIMES"

VEGA-TABLES (B.WILSON/V.D.PARKS)
"MRS O'LEARY'S COW"
"LOVE TO SAY DA DA"
"SURF'S UP"

BIBLIOGRAPHY

Beach Boys pictures can be found on the following sites:
http://www,exclaim.ca/images/up-Beach-Boys.jpg
http://www.reactioary.century.files.wordpress.com/2009/03/the-beach-boys.jpg
http://solarnavigator.net/music_images/beach_boys_group_photo.jpg
http://jason.steadypc.net/Pictures/beach-boys-the-photo-beach-boys-6233594.jpg

Summer Days (and Summer Nights):
http://www.surfermoon.com/lyrics/summer_ days.html

Ultimate Christmas: http://www.surfermoon.com/lyrics/ultchristmas.html

Christmas Album: http://www.surfermoon.com/lyrics/christmas.html

Concert: http://www.surfermoon.com/lyrics/concert.html

All Summer Long: http://www.surfermoon.com/lyrics/all_summer_long.html

Shut Down Volume II: http://www.surfermoon.com/lyrics/shut_down_vol2.html

Friends: http://www.surfermoon.com/lyrics/friends.html

Wild Honey: http://www.surfermoon.com/lyrics/wild_ honey.html

Smiley Smile: http://www.surfermoon.com/lyrics/smiley_ smile.html

Pet Sounds: http://www.surfermoon.com/lyrics/pet_ sounds.html

Recorded "Live" at a Beach Boys' Party!:
http://www.surfermoon.com/lyrics/party.html

Today: http://www.surfermoon.com/lyrics/today.html

Looking Back With Love:
http://www.surfermoon.com/lyrics/looking_back_with_love.html

Pacific Ocean Blue:
http://www.surfermoon.com/lyrics/pacific_ocean_blue.html

Like A Brother: http://www.surfermoon.com/lyrics/like _a _brother.html

Youngblood (Carl Wilson):
http://www.surfermoon.com/lyrics/youngblood.html

Carl Wilson (Carl Wilson):
http://www.surfermoon.com/lyrics/carl_wilson.html

Miscellaneous Brian Wilson Tracks:
http://www.surfermoon.com/lyrics/miscellaneousbw.html

That Lucky Old Sun:
http://www.surfermoon.com/lyrics/that_lucky_old_sun.html

What I Really Want For Christmas (Brian Wilson):
http://www.surfermoon.com/lyrics/what_i_really_want_for_christmas.ht
ml

Smile (Brian Wilson): http://www.surfermoon.com/lyrics/smile.html

Getting' In Over My Head (Brian Wilson):
http://www.surfermoon.com/lyrics/gettin_in_over_my_head.html

Brian Wilson Presents Pet Sound Live:
http://www.surfermoon.com/lyrics/pet_sounds_live.html

Live At The Roxy (Brian Wilson):
http://www.surfermoon.com/lyrics/live_at_the_roxy_2.html

Little Deuce Coupe:
http://www.surfermoon.com/lyrics/little_deuce_coupe.html

Surfer Girl: http://www.surfermoon.com/lyrics/surfer_girl.html

Surfin' U.S.A: http://www.surfermoon.com/lyrics/surfin_usa.html

Surfin' Safari: http://www.surfermoon.com/lyrics/surfin_safari.html

Live At The Roxy (Brian Wilson): http://www.surfermoon.com/lyrics/
live_at_the_roxy_1.html

Imagination (Brian Wilson):
http://www.surfermoon.com/lyrics/imagination.html

The Wilsons (Carnie and Wendy Wilson):
http://www.surfermoon.com/lyrics/the_wilsons.html

Orange Crate Art (Van Dyke Park with Brian Wilson):
http://www.surfermoon.com/lyrics/orange_crate_art.html

I Just Wasn't Made For These Times (Brian Wilson):
http://www.surfermoon.com/lyrics/ijwmftt.html

Brian Wilson: http://www.surfermoon.com/lyrics/brian_wilson.html

Summer in Paradise:
http://www.surfermoon.com/lyrics/summer_in_paradise.html

Still Cruisin': http://www.surfermoon.com/lyrics/still_cuisinn.html

Beach Boys (1985):
http://www.surfermoon.com/lyrics/beach_boys_85.html

Keepin' The Sumer Alive:
http://www.surfermoon.com/lyrics/keepin_the_summer_alive.html

L.A.(Light Album):):
http://www.surfermoon.com/lyrics/light_album.html

M.I.U. Album: http://www.surfermoon.com/lyrics/miu.html

The Beach Boys Love You:
http://www.surfermoon.com/lyrics/love_you.html

15 Big Ones: http://www.surfermoon.com/lyrics/15_big_ones.html

In Concert (1972-73): http://www.surfermoon.com/lyrics/inconcert.html

Mount Vernon and Fairway:
http://www.surfermoon.com/lyrics/mt_vernon.html

Holland: http://www.surfermoon.com/lyrics/holland.html

Carl and The Passions-so Tough:
http://www.surfermoon.com/lyrics/so_tough.html

Surf's Up: http://www.surfermoon.com/lyrics/surfs_up.html

Sunflower: http://www.surfermoon.com/lyrics/sunflower.html

Miscellaneous Beach Boys Tracks:
http://www.surfermoon.com/lyrics/miscellaneous.html

Spring (Marilyn Wilson and Diane Rovell):
http://www.surfermoon.com/lyrics/spring.html

Pet Projects: The Brian Wilson Productions:
http://www.surfermoon.com/lyrics/pet_projects.html

Bonus tracks 1962-1965: http://www.surfermoon.com/lyrics/bonus_62-65.html

Bonus tracks 1966-1969: http://www.surfermoon.com/lyrics/bonus_66-69.html

20/20: http://www.surfermoon.com/lyrics/20-20.html

Sweet Insanity (Brian Wilson):
http://www.surfermoon.com/lyrics/sweet_insanity.html

Good Vibrations: Thirty Years Of The Beach Boys Disc 1:
http://www.surfermoon.com/lyrics/box_set_1.htm

Good Vibrations: Thirty Years Of The Beach Boys Disc 2:
http://www.surfermoon.com/lyrics/box_set_2.htm

Good Vibrations: Thirty Years Of The Beach Boys Disc3:
http://www.surfermoon.com/lyrics/box_set_3.htm

Good Vibrations: Thirty Years Of The Beach Boys Disc 4:
http://www.surfermoon.com/lyrics/box_set_4.htm

Box Set Bonus Disc:
http://www.surfermoon.com/lyrics/box_set_bonus.htm

The Sixties…The Seventies, Eighties. and Nineties Other Beach
Boys…Brian Wilson Solo Albums And Projects…Other Solo Albums…
Unreleased albums: http://www.surfermoon.com/lyrics.shtml

ABOUT THE AUTHOR

I was 59 years old; a mother of three very special and supportive children and a grandmother of three wonderful grandsons (I now have five grand-children.) when I started writing my first book whilst watching a Bon Jovi concert DVD. (I am an avid fan, if you can call me that; crazy is more like it.)

I write from the heart and I really enjoyed writing the book, so I wrote another using a different artist, and the books kept coming to me and I kept writing them.(with a little help from above.)

Because I use different artist/artists song titles I have to be very careful with Copyright so a lot of legal requirements have to be taken into consideration before publishing the books. I also needed a name that would connect my books to each other; so the "Song Title Series" books began.

All my books are short stories; however it depends on how many song titles there are to be used, as to the length of the book. Some artists didn't have enough song titles on their own so I combined them with a few other artists. Other artists had that many song titles that I could have written a novel; but it would have ended up being boring.

Challenges I like, so writing books with various artists are a lot of fun and need careful thinking.

Why should I have all the fun writing the books and not be able to share them with everyone; so I have converted them into large print books so that you can share my fun as well.

Hopefully in the not too distant future; the books will also be available as audio books so that no-one will miss out on my fun and enjoyment of writing these unique books. I hope that you enjoy reading them.

My web site www.songtitleseries.com is the place to visit for updates of new books and the place to purchase other titles in all formats.

TESTIMONIALS

After reading through your range of books I felt I must compliment you Joan on the imaginative and entertaining way in which you presented each group and the Musicians in those groups. The way the stories were constructed is a credit to your work ethic. These must have taken considerable time to piece together and it is obviously a work of love for you.
I wish you all the success you truly deserve and look forward to seeing you next time you visit Tamworth.
Peter Harkins
Managing Director Cheapa Music
Country Music Capital Tamworth

The song titles series are books that were intriguing and were hard to believe that these short stories were written within the incorporated song titles of the artists that are mentioned in the titles. I loved what I have read so far and think that anyone with an imagination and love of music as the author you will surely enjoy reading these.
L.K. Brisbane Australia.

Joan Maguire Books are very nice, I enjoy reading them so much, they are hard to put down!! Especially when she does one about Bonjovi and their songs!!!
If I can say, it is worth every penny, when you buy one!!! The Books make nice presents, for a person whom loves to read!!! I can guarantee that you will LOVE these books, because I do!!!!!!!!!
Dawn from Newark, Delaware in the United States of America

I am Susie and would like to tell you guys, how much I am enjoying Joan Maguire's Books!! They are very enjoyable, and they are something that you do not ever want to put down!! I really enjoy these books; I can't wait until the next one that she puts out!!!!!!! I say go to your local book store, today and get one, you will not be disappointed!!!!!
Sue-from the United States of America

www.ingramcontent.com/pod-product-compliance
Lightning Source LLC
Chambersburg PA
CBHW062026040426
42447CB00010B/2159